Research Games:

An approach to the Study of Decision Processes

Research Games:

An approach to the Study of Decision Processes

K. C. BOWEN

with contributions by
JANET I. HARRIS

ORASA text No. 3

Taylor & Francis · London

Halsted Press
(a division of John Wiley & Sons Inc.)
New York · Toronto

1978

First published 1978 by Taylor & Francis Ltd, London
and Halsted Press (a division of John Wiley & Sons Inc.), New York

Taylor & Francis ISBN 0 85066 169 2

Printed and bound in the United Kingdom by
Taylor & Francis (Printers) Ltd
Rankine Road, Basingstoke, Hampshire RG24 0PR

Library of Congress Cataloging in Publication Data

Bowen, Kenneth Crewdson
  Research games

  (ORASA text; no. 3)
  "A Halsted Press book"
  Bibliography: p.
  Includes index
  1. Game theory.   2. Research—Methodology.   3. Decision-making.
I. Harris, Janet I., joint author.   II. Title.   III. Series: Orasa text; no. 3.
QA269.B68   1979   00.4'24   78–12363
ISBN 0–470–26535–3

Contents

Introduction by the Editor

The use of war games as a means of exploring and evaluating military strategy and tactics was established long before Operational Research and Systems Analysis came into being. From the earliest days of military OR, however, gaming has been seen as an OR activity, and it has remained so since. Yet, despite its long history, gaming has not developed as a subject in the way that one might have expected, and its transfer into civilian life has been most disappointing. One of the possible reasons for this may lie in the fact that because it existed before the analysts came along, the technique has never been subjected to the kind of specific scrutiny that every other OR tool has received. When gaming techniques have proved inadequate, it has perhaps been too easy to explore some alternative such as computer simulation, though they do not serve the same purposes. Moreover, the widespread use of elaborate management games, all too many of which should be classed as educational entertainment, has diverted attention away from the unique features that gaming offers to the serious analyst.

Ken Bowen's book is an attempt to help reverse that trend. It does not attempt to be authoritative, but rather to suggest ways in which Gaming can be used as a research tool. At the same time it reviews the slender literature in this field, which should be of considerable value to the newcomer to the field. There appears to be a reviving interest in the scientific use of operational gaming at the present time, and it is hoped that this volume will be a useful contribution to that development.

JANUARY 1978   R. C. TOMLINSON

Foreword

My interest in games for research purposes started some fifteen years ago. So that the reader can judge whether any initial bias has coloured this account of my present views, I should admit that my interest was generated by doubts as to whether large-scale games, of the type popular with military operational research groups in the early 1960s, were capable of providing results which could be tested in a manner appropriate to a would-be scientific tool. Since then, I have realized that results from most operational research models are very difficult to 'validate' in anything like the same way that the results of scientific, and repeatable, experiments on real-world phenomena can be validated. My fears, rather than being assuaged, have thus been extended to all models that ape the real world too closely in the richness and variety of their variables and relationships, especially when the behaviour of people is included.

This monograph is largely an account of work which has been done during the past six years. The material of chapter 2 has previously been widely circulated as an informal DOAE Research Working Paper, No. CC5, July 1972, but since then important changes have been made to the matrix headings under which the purposes of the games are classified. Chapter 4 and much of chapter 6 was issued as DOAE Memorandum 7117, June 1971, *The Structure and Classification of Operational Research Games*, which has also had wide circulation; it is not changed in essence, but there are editing variations and some new observations, mainly of a descriptive nature. The material of chapters 3 and 5 has also been issued before, in the ways which are described in chapter 5.

No-one suddenly produces ideas: they come as a response to external stimuli. So I will offer my thanks, first, to Dr Andrew Stratton who asked deceptively simple questions about the place of games among the many operational research techniques. His interest in the resulting paper led to many more questions and to discussions with users and potential users of games both within and outside the defence field. I also acknowledge the importance of game developments by R. P. (Paul) Rose and Paul M. Sutcliffe in the later 1960s. Working in a Maritime OR Group, of which I was superintendent, they produced the Submarine Approach Game. This is one of the most successful games that I know of, and it is the prototype of similar games now being developed for the study of information and decision in Army 'Command and Control' organizations.

There are many others who have contributed to my education. This is not to say that I have borrowed ideas from them directly, or that I have been convinced by argument on contentious issues. It is, primarily,that they have been influential in the gaming world by the clarity of what they have written, by their skills in producing and playing games, and by their enthusiasm for the subject. I will name three of these: Dr M. Weiner of the RAND Corporation, who introduced me to open, 'seminar', games; Professor R. W. Shephard of the Royal Military College of Science, Shrivenham, who, more than anyone else I know, has striven to bring large-scale gaming closer towards the elusive research category; and Professor M. Shubik, who has contributed much of great value to the literature and has made encouraging remarks about the research on games which I have carried out or controlled. I should add that, in this last case, there are undoubtedly differences in our attitudes to some aspects of classification and theory, but, as will be apparent from the appendix, respect is mutual.

I am grateful to the Operational Research Society for the opportunity to put my ideas into a single publication. Needless to say, not all of 'my ideas' were originally mine: my thanks are especially due to my research colleague, Janet I. Harris, for her agreement to my using, for chapters 3 and 5, an account by her of a study of the concepts of a conflict game, work which she carried out in the framework of my overall research programme. She has also helped greatly with the major task of editing the penultimate draft and with the proof-reading of the finished work. Another valuable commentary on an early draft came from Rachel Bodle of the Operational Research Executive, National Coal Board, the direction of whose own work on games is of general interest and importance.

Finally, I thank the editor of this series, whose interest in games led him to invite me to be an author of one of the early publications, and whose advice has been of great value to me in its preparation. Rolfe Tomlinson has stimulated and encouraged work on games at the National Coal Board (Operational Research Executive) and he led the discussion sessions on gaming at the first of the Lancaster–Sussex–Pennsylvania Universities Discussion Conferences, at Oxford in August 1971. If, through any interest created by this monograph, games can be made to serve operational research in a more fundamental way, it is perhaps fitting that it should occur under the aegis of a Past-President, who has done so much for the Society and for operational research.

K. C. BOWEN

1. Introduction and summary

1.1 General

This monograph gives a personal view of what uses can be made of games and of how games should be developed. It concentrates on the types of game that can be used to model systems which exhibit purposeful behaviour. The researcher who uses a game is interested, directly or indirectly, in the behaviour of the people within such systems; the decisions which they make will generally have important effects on the performance of the systems.

No theories of gaming are established here, although most of what is said seems likely to be important for the development of such theory. The survey of games which is offered is also far from complete: the use of games for research and other purposes is widespread, and, even during the writing of this monograph, the author has found more subject areas in which games are now being played. The examples of games which are included are mainly those which have been used in operational research; some of these seem to have been basically unsuitable for research in its strictest sense, although they may well have been instrumental in providing some measure of understanding of the systems they modelled.

Without a detailed specification of some problem, only a rough guide can be provided as to what sort of modelling might succeed or fail. In practice, the introduction of a game in the course of research studies may not be for the central purpose of the research. A game may be a means of obtaining some idea of the decision problems involved in operating within a complicated system. It may be used to give confirmation, in the mind of a customer, of the sort of results obtained from less overt, and less realistic, computer simulations or mathematical models. But a game as a research model should offer more than this. It should enable theories, involving the behaviour of people, to be tested. It should enable statements to be made on the basis of systematic analysis, with explicit understanding of the underlying assumptions. It follows that such a model must be controllable, as must any good research model. It is this need for control that limits the usefulness for research of many types of game.

White, in his work on *Decision Methodology*[1], stresses the need for models to be controlled in the sense used here. The user of the model must know explicitly which variables have produced the various observed effects on the solutions of the model. Neither models nor solutions can be invariant with time; the system modelled, the criteria for decision, and the environment are subject to change. Unless there is control, the solutions of a model cannot be adequately interpreted in the real world. If a model includes the behaviour of people, control becomes more difficult, since the characteristics of decisions are much less well understood than are the results of an interaction within a mechanical system. The consequence, as will be seen, is that games for research purposes cannot yet adequately treat complex decision sequences.

Games, particularly for military purposes, have been played in many forms over the centuries. The story of what has been done, albeit fascinating, has no place here. A brief account of what H. G. Wells[2] wrote about as *Little Wars*, the playing through of battles using small-scale models of terrain, vehicles and men, can be found in a 1970 issue of the *Illustrated London News*[3]. Such games are still popular and their adherents would regard the alternative expression 'toy wars' as derogatory, since they are played for purposes no less serious than those of many political and management games.

The same account discusses some of the then current uses of games of 'crisis' situations in political and social science teaching, and gives examples of some of the more elaborate games that can be devised to enable people to exercise their powers of decision in roles otherwise not experienced by them. However, the insight gained from such games, valuable though it may be for individual players, does not provide explicit data which can be easily analysed.

Nevertheless, since gaming is not a new technique, games having been used extensively by operational researchers over the past three decades, it might seem that the obvious course to take here would be to review a selection of the games that have been played, to comment on their strengths and weaknesses, and their successes and failures, and, finally, to generalise from this to indicate the way ahead. Unfortunately, especially in the United Kingdom, there is a dearth of adequate records of game-playing. For various reasons involving confidentiality, case histories with actual data inputs and outputs are not available. A contributory cause, no doubt, is the sheer size of the recording task, a problem which is not unfamiliar to those who develop large-scale computer simulations.

It is believed that size and complexity alone have led to most games' being unsuited to their stated purpose of research. It will be necessary to inquire what a reduction in this size and complexity would imply. The purpose of a game may, of course, not be research, and this will be seen to make a difference to what can be permitted in the way of detailed representation.

1.2 The nature of a game

Before summarising the aspects of game playing that will be discussed in the following chapters, it is necessary to be more specific about what is meant by a 'game'. The word implies that it has something of the nature of a typical recreational game. The picture is of a number of people, acting individually or in groups, in a competitive situation. They have resources which they can dispose of according to rules, dealing with such things as losses and gains. Their 'moves' may be simultaneous or sequential. They develop strategies for winning and they make and implement decisions. A game need not, but often does, possess some of the attributes of a 'real' situation. But this is not enough to define a game in the present context.

A game will be played for some purpose. If the game is to be of operational use, the purpose will be to develop some understanding of the way in which purposeful behaviour can affect the situations occurring in the game. These situations will model real situations in which an individual wishes to be able to make more informed choices —to deploy his resources to better advantage or to acquire new and different resources. A game therefore needs to have a model of the systems involved and of the environment of these systems. The similarity of this model to the real world must suit the nature of the inquiry into the situations and the choices involved.

The real-world decision-makers may or may not participate in a game. If they do not, they must be represented adequately for its purpose. When a game is being played, the nature of the model changes. What was a purely mechanistic model, responding only to time, now incorporates a model of the decision-making process, and will also respond to the decision-maker's behaviour. The former model required rules only to represent changes in the situation which were independent of the players' interaction with it. The latter model must also have rules to represent the consequences of decision, namely, changes to the dynamics of the situation represented by the model of the systems and their environment. There must also be ways of letting the players have data, not necessarily complete, to describe the new situation.

1.3 Classification of purpose and structure of a game

In chapter 2, the broad purposes of games will be discussed in order to identify some of their essential characteristics. One category will be games for research. Such games will generally be played to obtain measures which describe the decision-process and the relationships between situations, choices and consequences. Those who control the game must ensure that they understand, as fully as possible, not only the way in which the model of the situation works, but also how it is perceived by the players, what characteristics of the game affect decisions, and how decisions affect the situation. These aspects will be the subject matter of chapters 3 and 5.

Chapter 4 discusses the various structures of research games that can be considered. Games in which representations of decision-processes are used, even though human players are not involved, will be included. The representation of decision-processes must not be arbitrary. Indeed, such a representation will usually be obtained from a research game which examines human choice-behaviour. Sometimes, it will be based on real-world observations. In either case, the representation may be either stochastic or deterministic, depending on what appears to be suitable for the purpose of the inquiry. It will be suggested therefore that both computer simulations and analytical models may have sufficient direct relevance to research into decision-making for them to be regarded as games. It is essential to this use of the word 'game' that the appropriateness of the representation, including the effects that any assumptions have on model outputs, has been considered and made explicit.

It is apparent that there are three important levels at which purpose can be discussed. First, there is the broad or primary purpose, for example research or teaching or recreation, which is dealt with by a classification developed in chapter 2. This purpose being clear, the question then is what is wanted from the particular game. Chapter 3 discusses this, particularly what aspects of the decision-process might be studied and what the variables might be in a sequence of games. In a sense, what is provided is a clarification, rather than a classification, of the more detailed purpose of those who control the game. Chapter 4 provides a classification of some 100 different structures of games which might be relevant to this purpose. The classification was developed for the purpose of categorising research games, although, as will be seen, it can be applied to games played for other primary purposes.

Classification is an underrated 'measurement' technique. It lies between verbal or pictorial description and ordering (or ranking). In its most useful form, it is a dichotomous process, as in chapters 2 and 4. Here, it helps to identify and use characteristics on which useful descriptions of games can be based. It provides a framework which may identify types of game which might not otherwise have been thought of. It enables conceptually similar games to be seen as such, even though, because of the language of the situations they examine, or because of the level of complexity of strategy they involve (assuming this level not to be a factor of the classification), they may seem to be very different. It also enables something to be said about the degree of difficulty of control of games of different structure; although strictly this can only be done in relation to the distinctions which are used in the classification, somewhat wider inferences may be made in practice.

But, above all, classification enables a number of very useful distinctions to be made without the need for absolute measurement, or with a minimum of such measurement. As will be seen, particularly with regard to the classification of structure in chapter 4, absolute measurement of variables may be very difficult or, at present, impossible. This relates particularly to variables which concern human behaviour.

1.4 The construction and playing of research games

Because conflict, in the most general sense, is an essential ingredient of any decision-process, chapter 3 introduces and defines the concepts of conflict and crisis. Various other concepts, such as aim, policy and action, are also defined. Chapter 5 returns to these concepts and discusses the primary issues in the construction and playing of one of the simplest of the types of research game identified in chapter 4. This game was originally described as a conflict game. The logic of such a game was developed in order to study how to control a game to yield data which could be used to resolve or avoid conflict in the sort of situations for which the game might be played. The arguments are very general and it does seem that most of what is in chapter 5 is relevant to any research game which uses human players and which aims to analyse their responses to situations and information.

The roles of the experimenter (who controls the model of the situation; the players themselves; and the game as a whole which includes the interaction of the players with the situation) are necessarily mentioned in chapters 2 and 4, although not in great detail. In chapter 5, not only the role of the experimenter, but also that of the 'game-maker', is thoroughly explored. The game-maker is the person who constructs the game for a defined purpose. The experimenter tries to produce results relevant to that purpose; although he does not choose the game, he will be responsible for the choice of players and for their control. Logically, it is undesirable that game-maker and experimenter be one person. The reasons are similar to those which inhibit an experimenter's being a player in the game, except in certain exploratory stages in its development.

1.5 The literature on games

As stated earlier, not many British games have been documented in very useful ways. Those games which are commented on in this monograph are not therefore the subject of a chapter, but are described briefly, at suitable points in the text, to illustrate the sort of game which is being discussed. References to available documents, or to the individuals or organizations who have developed games, are also given.

Some of the general references are to the US literature, and one is to the Canadian literature. What use is being made of games in any other countries is not known to the author. The US literature has fortunately been most adequately surveyed by Shubik[4-8]. Short summaries of, and comments on, his work are given in the appendix. Shubik also covers what he sees as the more important contributions from other countries.

It might be expected that some papers or books on the uses of games would have emerged as a result of the teaching of operational research in the universities of the United Kingdom. As far as is known, there are none. If any exist, they are well hidden. Indeed, there seems to be negligible attention paid to the playing of games, as opposed to game theory, in the formal teaching of operational research techniques. The author has given seminars, based on the material in this book, in various British universities. His being invited to do so was based on the principle that during their course of study, students ought to learn that such models *might* be useful, or at least to know that they exist.

The references are reasonably comprehensive for the limited aims of this monograph as stated at the outset. If anything important is omitted, it is not from lack of interest or energy, since the author has been seeking material on games for many years. Nevertheless, there are some notable and deliberate omissions. Very few references to the considerable literature on games for fun, management games and game theory are given. These subjects are dealt with in chapter 6, and the following three sections give reasons for the brevity of this later treatment.

1.6 Games for fun

The discussion of games that most people have experienced to some degree during their childhood, and since, will be confined to how they can be described in terms of the classification of the structure of games given in chapter 4. The phrase 'games for fun' has been used in order to avoid the word 'recreation' which is more generally related to physical activities (sports). It is shown that the classification is applicable to games for fun, and does identify groups of games which are conceptually similar, even though these similarities may come as a surprise. More importantly, by examining the sequence of game playing through which a child develops his or her skill at games, some guidance is given for seeking a similar sequence for the development of research games.

Some readers may feel that a more thorough examination of some of the more elaborate games for fun could help to provide ideas about rules, about player perceptions of 'reality', and so on. The author does not believe that such an approach would be profitable, because games for fun lack the control which research games, on which this monograph concentrates, require. Mention is made, in chapter 2, of a step towards developing research games from games for fun, and it may be that, in due course, there will be incentives to examine the latter more deeply.

1.7 Management games

Management games are also played under very loose control and, despite their richness of detail, have more kinship with games for fun than with research games. Nevertheless, because they contain more convincing models of real-world systems, they are inherently more likely to be capable of development into research games. Furthermore, some are closely associated with the operational research process, and almost all might be useful to operational researchers, and others, as a means of acquainting themselves better with the working of the systems which are modelled, or with the difficulties of the decision-process. Some management games are produced by operational researchers not as part of their research, but simply because of their skills as model-builders.

A few management games are discussed briefly in chapter 6 to underline these points. The literature describing them is referenced. The applicability of the classification of games according to their structure (chapter 4) is again illustrated.

1.8 Game theory

Game theory is not, unfortunately, a theory of the games with which this monograph is concerned. There is, however, a vast literature on simple, experimental, non-zero-sum games (mainly based on 2×2 strategy matrices) which are used to examine or to develop theories of behaviour. They are closely associated with game-theoretic models, but there are difficulties in relating the results of such games to real-world situations. At present, they are, at best, a means of getting some ideas about conflict or competitive situations: they do not provide input data for operational models. Zero-sum game theory can also provide a framework for thinking about certain situations, but the models it uses are oversimplified and of limited value for operational research studies.

Game theory is therefore treated briefly. The classification of chapter 4 is used, however, to make clear the distinction between game-theoretic models considered as games, and experimental games based on game-theoretic concepts. Those who wish to extend their knowledge of what has been done in game-playing in this context must read, at some length, elsewhere.

It is hoped that the link between game theory and games will become stronger. Reference is made, in chapter 6, to papers describing recent research at the University of Sussex on behaviour in conflict situations. This stemmed from earlier, and important, work at the University of Pennsylvania, also referenced. The Sussex research has now moved in a new direction and is beginning to cast serious doubts on earlier behavioural theories developed through experimental games. It is not yet possible to review usefully what impact this work may have on games in general.

A source which provides a useful coverage of game-theory in relation to gaming is one of the books by Shubik[7] discussed in the appendix. It is accepted, as Shubik points out, that the literature of game theory introduces concepts and treatments of concepts, which can be useful to those who play games. So of course does the literature that deals conceptually with communication, information, conflict, decision and many other subjects. In the space available here, detailed treatment of these subjects, as well as treatment of game theory, must be omitted.

1.9 The future

The final chapter addresses the future of gaming. Although this is necessarily tentative, it stems from many years of research by the author and his close associates in gaming and allied topics. For those who are game enthusiasts, it is an encouraging message. Despite the present difficulties of designing and playing research games, these games are seen not just as an important class of operational research models, but as models essential to the *science* of operational research, seen as a science of decision-making processes.

What is offered here, then, is not by any means a 'compleat gamer' treatise. There is not yet anything which can be taken, with assurance, as '*the* way forward'. There is no established 'technique' as there is for queueing, linear programming, stock control, simulation, and so on. This monograph concentrates on an approach to a theory of gaming, although the title is more cautious. The author may well be attacked for his pessimism, or his optimism, depending on the reader. Any such positive response will be welcome: there is a great deal to be done, as those who read on will discover.

2. The purposes of games

2.1 A broad classification

There are two well-established purposes for games, other than that of research. Games can be used for teaching purposes and games can be used for fun. In both cases, some explanation is needed to avoid confusion of language.

Teaching implies the putting over of facts, or theories, or, in some cases, hypotheses which are currently used as a guide for action. A teaching game is therefore a model of some part of the real world, within which a student can be guided to see why his behaviour might be 'right' or 'wrong'. The game is controlled by the teacher so that the desired events occur and so that the consequences of behaviour can be analysed to demonstrate the principle being taught. The student is, of course, free to question the teaching; both he and the teacher may become aware of possible new concepts, but this aspect is not a primary reason for the game as a *teaching* medium.

Games for *fun* are defined here as mental exercises, *not* physical ones (this will be commented on further in chapter 4). People playing such games choose to do so for motives which are, generally, those of interest in recreational mental activity. Games for fun are not invented to meet a clearly defined demand. They are on offer to those who choose to play. This contrasts with teaching games which are designed for specific groups with specific needs, and whose players are, generally, designated as such by the teacher.

Research games have different things in common with each of the other two types of games. As with teaching games, research games need control (by an experimenter) so that the behaviour of players can be made explicit. However, with research games, as with games for fun, the players come to the game because it cannot fulfil its function without them. Although it will need to call on players with appropriate experience for the decision-problems presented, the research game is not designed for a particular group of individuals. So far, we can formulate a classification in an incomplete matrix as in figure 2.1.

		SELECTION OF PLAYERS	
		Game designed to meet the needs of a specific group of people	Suitable people are found to play the game
?	Play controlled to make the players' behaviour explicit	TEACHING	RESEARCH
	?	?	FUN

FIGURE 2.1 A stage in the classification of games for different purposes.

There are three gaps in the table so constructed. The second row heading and the overall heading for rows need to be chosen and a fourth type of game should then become apparent.

It seems obvious that the second row should deal with games in which the players are not controlled, but play freely to extract something for themselves. Their behaviour will be known, to some extent, by themselves, but it will not be the purpose of the game to make this behaviour explicit for the information of anyone else. The fourth game is already defined as having been created for a specified group. Several such games exist in training establishments and have been called *teaching* games, although very few are covered by the harder definition of teaching that is used here. They do in fact offer a model world in which players can gain experience which, it is hoped, is relevant to their real-world needs. The only control that is exercised is that provided by the situations which are modelled and by the rules of the game. Those who administer the game may know what happens but have no clear means by which they can analyse, other than in a crude and highly subjective manner, the behaviour of the players.

Such a game will be called a *learning* game. It will have considerable value in its own right and may well be useful to researchers who seek insights into situations which they could otherwise never experience but only conceptualise (this does *not*, however, make such a game a research game). We can now complete the matrix of figure 2.1 and produce, as in figure 2.2, a 2 × 2 classification of games. The rows are shown as relating to the control of players.

		SELECTION OF PLAYERS	
		Game designed to meet the needs of a specific group of people	Suitable people are found to play the game
CONTROL OF PLAYERS	Play controlled to make the players' behaviour explicit	TEACHING ←——→ RESEARCH	
	Play unrestricted subject only to game rules and format	LEARNING ←——→ FUN	

FIGURE 2.2 A 2×2 classification of games for different purposes.

Figure 2.2 also shows certain connections between these types of game. The solid arrows imply that there are close similarities between games across columns. Research games seem likely to offer a framework for good teaching games; indeed, development of teaching games may require the earlier research process. Learning games must be fun in order to attract and motivate the player.

The dotted arrows imply more tenuous connections. A teaching game does not inhibit a learning process, although this is not the main aim. In the same way, a learning game can be usefully extended into the teaching mode, albeit with caution and without dogmatism,

by a teacher who has himself played the game. Clearly, the classification is not rigid: a game could be a deliberate cross between a
teaching and a learning game. The connection between research
games and games for fun is also of some importance. A research
game will impose constraints on players and on allowable situations:
unless these constraints are accepted by each player, despite his
awareness of his role as decision-maker in the real as well as the
model world, the game will be disrupted. The players must therefore be willing to play the game, just as it is, as they would a game for
fun.

All these links imply that there is considerable scope for
changing the purpose of a game by modifications in the selection and
control of players. There would, however, be consequent changes to
the structure of the game. Recent research at Sussex University[9]
indicates that some games for fun, such as 'Diplomacy', are sufficiently 'real' to be classified as learning games and, further, that they
can be modified to provide teaching and research games for the
study of behaviour in conflict situations. The potential importance of
this, in relation to increasing the richness of description of the
decision situation, will be referred to again in chapter 7.

2.2 Other approaches to classification

The genesis of the classification of figure 2.2 did not in fact follow
the direct deductive path given here. There were jumps in the logical
processes described, and the final labelling of the characteristics of
the game is different and, it is hoped, more precise than in earlier
versions (see the reference in the Foreword and that relating to the
Wessex Management Game in chapter 4). Strictly, also, the learning
game was not 'discovered' in this way, although the realisation that
it was a fundamentally different concept to that of a teaching game
did not become explicit until the matrix was formed. The approach
to classification as described here was stimulated by work by Ackoff
and Emery[10] on the study of personality types.

There are of course other ways of classifying the purposes of
games. The commonest approach uses family trees, but, because this

does not necessarily concentrate on the dimensions involved, it may lead to unsatisfactory or unnecessary distinctions. Shubik[11] used such an approach in a 1972 paper and his findings had some arguable features. He deals with six purposes—*teaching, experimentation, entertainment, therapy and diagnosis, operations,* and *training.* His *entertainment* was what, here, has been called *fun,* except that he included sports (involving physical interactions). His *experimentation* related to 2 × 2 games, ones with a game-theoretic basis which are simple and widely-used forms of research games. *Operations,* as used by Shubik, is not completely defined, but is clearly a more narrow term than the research label of figure 2.2. 'Research', as used throughout this monograph, is intended to cover *all* research games that might be used, by operational researchers and others, and not only those that simulate the operations of complex systems. It may be as well to emphasise that, as was said in the introduction, operational research may need games that are *not* research games, and Shubik's 'operations' may perhaps be intended to cover some of these, as well.

Shubik's choice of *therapy and diagnosis* as a label runs into two difficulties. Firstly, the label does not clearly exclude the others in the list, in particular teaching and training. The classification is, therefore, ambiguous. Secondly, the label is associated with a special context, medicine, while the others have much broader contextual relevance, including a possible relevance to medicine. Thirdly, two processes are being confused. A study for 'diagnosis' must examine the decision-processes of the players. What must be determined is the nature of their problem and why they react in the ways observed. A research game is required. On the other hand, one type of therapy, group therapy, is a learning game in its own right: the experimenter can only manipulate the game format and environment when setting up the game. Any game which attempts to mix learning and research functions, whether by accident or design, seems likely to fall between two stools. A classification which mixes these functions seems likely to confuse.

Finally, *training* as discussed by Shubik seems to be a cross between teaching and learning, and the essential differences between the two processes do not seem to be treated. This does not imply that such games do not exist, nor that they do not have uses. Indeed, this brief discussion of Shubik's interesting approach (which seems to have been somewhat modified in more recent publications—see appendix) is intended solely to show that a 2 × 2 classification can be surprisingly powerful compared to a more extensive, but less systematic, tree structure.

2.3 Extending the classification

Whatever the primary purpose of a game, the question of what aspects of decision-making are exercised or examined is of importance, but a formal extension of the above classification that will discriminate between such secondary purposes seems likely to be very difficult. No such extension has been attempted. Extended classifications for specific applications may nevertheless prove useful and, provided that they are not used outside their intended context, should be encouraged. Reference will be made, in chapter 6, to Eilon's classification of business games, which is an example of a simple, specialised classification.

The following chapter will discuss concepts fundamental to research games, including the variables which can be manipulated in such games in order to extract information about the decision-process. This will give an adequate basis for the later development (chapter 5) of the logic for constructing a special type of game chosen on the basis of a classification of game structure (chapter 4). The categorisation of the types of information that can be extracted will, at the end of chapter 5, be put in the form of a classification of purpose, although this last cannot be taken, at present, as more than an indication of what may be possible.

It cannot be overemphasised that clarity of purpose, in games as in any other model construction, is essential to a successful research outcome. Much game playing, ostensibly for research, has, in the event, yielded little more than fun for the players. This is hardly surprising. Many of the large-scale 'research' games played have been, by accident, more suited for use as learning games, although not designed for such a purpose. The players have had enthusiasm for these game-worlds in which they could demonstrate their professional skill, and they have often been irritated by even the small measures of control that experimenters have sought to impose. Enthusiasm of players for a game can be misleading as to its value; a player in a research game should be giving rather than expecting to receive satisfaction, and too much enthusiasm for the game may be an indication that something is wrong. Control of the game for the purpose stated must be carefully maintained, lest the players take control for *their* purposes.

3. Some concepts involved in the decision-process

3.1 Conflict and crisis

In the situation which a game models, there is always a conflict present. Indeed, the need for decision implies that this is so. But it is not necessarily true that a better understanding of the nature of the conflict, of why it arose and of how it might be resolved, is the purpose of playing a particular game. It is more often the case that, given that the conflict exists, it is required to know how best 'we' can use our resources in order to 'win'. What is meant by 'winning' is, however, necessarily related to the particular underlying conflict.

For the purpose of a research game, the associated concepts of 'conflict' and 'crisis' are relevant. To be useful, they must have an operational definition. It is assumed that, in normal usage, 'conflict' is something arising from the interaction between two or more systems, and 'crisis' is a situation perceived by a system as one of unusual or unexpected threat to itself—often associated with conflict—whose handling is not routine. Conflict and crisis are generally discussed in the context of their effects on the general purposeful behaviour of a system. This behaviour may be defined in terms of three concepts:

(1) an *aim* of a system, which is a future condition of itself or its environment which the system desires to bring about;
(2) a *policy* of a system, which is a plan of action intended to bring about one or more of the system's aims; and
(3) an *action* of a system, which can be any action taken in the process of implementing a policy.

Given these defined concepts, two systems may be said to be in *conflict* with each other if any of their respective aims, policies or actions are mutually incompatible. This does not seem to diverge too far. from what is normally understood by 'conflict', but two things should be noted. Firstly, a purposeful system can be in conflict with a non-purposeful system, such as a mechanical system or Nature; in such a case, it is only the *action* of the non-purposeful system that has meaning, and the concepts of aim and policy can be regarded as being subsumed in the action. Secondly, the inclusion of aims and policies in the definition means that the period of build-up towards an actual collision of activities is also counted as a stage of conflict. Of course, this definition also makes it possible for a system to perceive itself as being in conflict when an outside observer might think otherwise, but there is no apparent reason why conflict should not be partly subjective. This may be even more true of crisis. In general use, 'crisis' tends to imply a situation of special risk, probably in the course of a conflict, over which the system is at least temporarily in a state of indecision. In terms of the system's purposeful behaviour, as described above, this risk must imply that the system's aims, or policies, seem likely to be frustrated. This in itself need not always lead to crisis. If it is only the system's actions or policies that are blocked, then it may be relatively easy for it to continue to pursue its existing aims by some change of plan, and crisis will not occur (even though outsiders may expect it to). If, however, the system's aims are being directly frustrated, or if it can find no acceptable alternative policy, then it will have no choice but to change its aims or to adopt a previously unacceptable policy, and before this can be done the system will experience *crisis* (sometimes of a very short term nature, but nevertheless a period of real anguish).

3.2 Need for a model which is a game with human players

A game with human players seems a suitable means of studying crisis because there are difficulties in using other, more obvious methods. Referring to past experience may not yield very much because crises, in the nature of things, are comparatively uncommon and also fairly individual. This means that historical data may be sparse, and not readily comparable between different incidents; it also means that the data needed to answer specific questions may be lacking. For similar reasons, expert opinion on crisis *in general* may be hard to find. This suggests that fresh data should be created experimentally. But full-scale experiment on real systems in crisis would be too dangerous, and, in any case, suitable conflicts might not be available. The obvious remaining course is to make small-scale, harmless experiments, leading to provisional conclusions, by modelling the real situation. Here, the subject-matter under study affects the type of model to be chosen.

If conflict and crisis are defined in terms of the purposeful behaviour of interacting systems, the model used must represent systems capable of having aims and formulating policies, and such systems typically involve people. Moreover, the presence or absence of people is crucial to the behaviour of any system, because people are essentially unpredictable even under apparently identical conditions. Hence their behaviour cannot initially be adequately represented in a completely inanimate model, but must be supplied by other people contributing to its working. The model then becomes a game incorporating human players. It will later be suggested that a model that contains a representation of decision processes can always be regarded as a game, even though it may not use human players. However, not until behaviour has become much better understood through games *with* human players can such representation be made in other than simple and potentially inaccurate ways.

3.3 Assumption: hierarchies

In describing the main features of interacting systems, their environment and their decision-making activities, a 'language' that draws attention to fundamental, recurring concepts is clearly desirable. Such a language should also be able to describe the games that model such systems. Purposeful behaviour by decision-makers in the real world should, if possible, be described in similar terms to the purposeful behaviour of those who play or control a game, and systems in the real world should be described so as to be comparable to their counterparts in any model. Whatever language is chosen should, as far as possible, be compact, unambiguous, and capable of under-lining similarities in and differences between the various concepts that are portrayed.

It is not possible to get away entirely from 'natural language', which is, in this case, the use of ordinary, non-technical English. A natural language is always needed, at least initially, to define any other 'language' that might be used. However, provided that the definitions needed are simple and few, translation between the two should not be difficult. The aim of the new language must be to give quicker and more useful insights into complicated system processes. In what follows, one initial assumption is made about the structure of real-world systems. This allows a simplification of the 'language' developed; it can be regarded as one of many permissible ways of describing the real world.

The assumption is that any real-world system which is to be modelled, or in which crisis is to be measured, is organized as a hierarchy. This means, as regards the structure of the system, that there are no partly overlapping subsystems; every pair of sub-systems either is disjoint, or has one subsystem completely con-tained in the other. It also means, as regards the behaviour of the system, that every subsystem has at least some influence over how its own subsystems behave. This in turn implies, among other things, that a subsystem in a hierarchy may possess aims acquired in two different ways—some dictated to it by the subsystem imme-diately containing it, and some of its own free choice (provided the latter are not incompatible with its compulsory aims).

The idea of a hierarchy can be illustrated using a diagrammatic notation[12] which will also be used to describe aspects of the structure of a game. For convenience, the conventions of this notation are summarised. A system is represented by a rectangular 'box' (figure 3.1), and containment of systems by a 'box within a box'. System interactions are shown by simple arrows, and these can obviously be inserted, in both directions, between any pair of systems of which one contains the other. Strictly speaking, this is the only kind of direct interaction between systems that is possible, and interactions between non-overlapping systems must be transmitted through some common containing system. It may be clearer, however, to show interactions that are felt to be important as taking place directly even between non-overlapping systems, and to omit any other interactions, direct or not, which are superfluous to the point being illustrated. Omission of interaction lines does *not* mean that interactions do not take place, only that attention is not being directed to them.

To make a diagram of this sort into a picture of a hierarchy (figure 3.2), one ensures that the diagram contains no partly over-lapping boxes, and includes only those interactions which represent an authoritative influence over other parts of the system. This leaves a diagram whose only interaction lines are between pairs of sub-systems contained one in the other, with only the downward half of the interaction inserted.

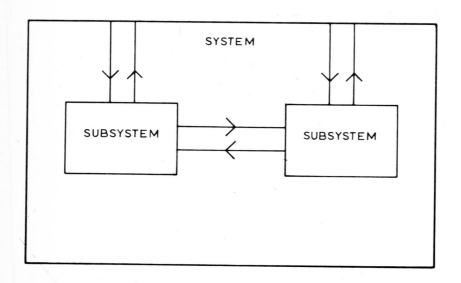

FIGURE 3.1 Systems.

3.4 Decisions

A *decision* made by the system is a conversion of

> aim into policy, or
>
> policy into action, or
>
> aim into action; or it is
>
> a selection of aims.

Thus, every purposeful subsystem in any system must make some decisions in the pursuit of its particular aims. If the system as a whole is a hierarchy, each of its subsystems will be able to include instructions to its own subsystems in any policy it formulates. Thus a

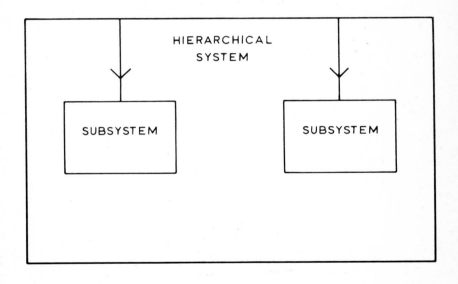

FIGURE 3.2 A hierarchy.

decision about policy at one level may impose some aims on sub-systems at the next lower level, requiring a new set of decisions on how to pursue these aims, and a branching chain of decisions is formed, descending from the largest system under study to the smallest of its subsystems. This process will be repeated as time goes on, as external conditions change, and the aims of the subsystems at different levels are either frustrated or achieved. Thus the whole progress of a conflict can be defined by a series of decisions taken at different levels within the system under study. These decisions are also the points at which the course of the conflict may possibly be altered by the system's own purposeful action, and so they may provide the framework on which a game should be built.

3.5 Measurement of crisis

The definition of *crisis* given earlier may be interpreted as meaning any point at which the system is unable to come to a *decision*, as defined above. This is in reasonable agreement with the circumstances generally associated with crisis. In any system, crises can obviously occur at quite low levels, when any subsystem faces a decision which it cannot reconcile with its aims. In a hierarchical system, however, even such a minor crisis may spread back up the chain of decisions on aims and policy to cause crises in successively larger subsystems, and even in the system as a whole. It may therefore be possible to measure the relative seriousness of a crisis within a particular hierarchy by the level at which it starts, and the number and level of the subsystems to which it spreads.

3.6 Construction of a game

The general purpose of a research game is to study the opportunities a system may have for controlling the course of a conflict in which it is involved. Any deliberate attempt to control the conflict must be associated with decisions on the part of the system as a whole and of its subsystems, and so such a game should explicitly include some occasions when decisions are to be taken. It will need to test the circumstances in which these decisions will work out satisfactorily for the system being studied. This suggests that a game might consist in playing through one or more points of decision in the course of a conflict, to see how differing inputs to the player affect the outcome. Since the entire conflict, developing over time, can be described in terms of a series of chains of such decisions, this approach should make it relatively easy to adjust the scope of a game according to requirements. This dwelling on specific points of decision is particularly appropriate to studies of more intense conflicts because the incidence and measurement of crisis are associated with taking or failing to take decisions; and also, since crisis involves the frustration of a system's currently held aims, it is reasonable to assume that a secondary aim in these decisions might be the avoidance of crisis in itself.

3.7 Variables

Assuming that the framework of a game, on whatever scale, will be a selection of the points of decision arising in the course of a particular conflict, several types of variable will be available for manipulation. They are

(1) the person actually playing the game;
(2) the precise information given to him (including reasonable variation in the system itself) for a given decision-point; and
(3) the decision-point itself (determined by the system level at which the decision is to be taken, and the stage in time of the conflict as a whole).

The choice of variables to be used will affect both the complexity of a game, and the type of conclusions that can be drawn from it. In the order of listing above, no variable can usefully be held fixed while one of those later in the list is allowed to vary; so a game using the later variables will inevitably be more complicated. This could also have its effect on the firmness of the conclusions drawn, since a simpler game, using only some of the earlier variables, would be easier to control. As to the kinds of information yielded by manipulating the respective variables, these would be

(1) prediction of the decision made for a rigidly specified situation;
(2) for a generally specified decision-situation, the effect on the decision of
    (a) the type, presentation and accuracy of the information given to the player and
    (b) the facilities and scope for action allowed to him in the game; and
(3) the manner of propagation through the system, and possible distortion, of
    (a) information and
    (b) aims and policies for the various subsystem levels.

Of these, the conclusions that can be derived from changing only the person playing the game would be too particular to be of much use. The simplest game that could give useful information of the other kinds listed above would, therefore, involve playing through a single decision-point with varying details of information about the decision-situation, and with various players.

It seems logical then to examine first the problems of playing such a simple game, but before the implications of such a course can be judged, it is necessary to consider a wider range of games. The simple game is certainly not the sort of game which has, traditionally, been played. The structure of possible games, and particularly the structure of games that have already been played, will therefore be examined. In this way, a more informed choice can be made of the type of game that it is possible to play usefully for the purpose of research into decision and conflict.

4. A classification of the structure of research games

4.1 The need for definition and classification

In operational research, particularly military operational research, large-scale games (games with decision-processes and the environment extensively represented) have been widely used. In the 1960s, the problems of the degree of control that could be imposed on such games had already raised doubts as to whether the games were adequate as research models. Questions that were asked included the following.

Were there simpler games that could help towards the same end?

Could the use of a computer simulation, for similar purposes, be regarded as a game, and, if so, were there important differences?

Was there any relationship between mathematical models and games?

What parameters could be selected to define, usefully, the nature of a game?

Would such definition help in selecting the right type of game to play?

The author attempted to answer some of these questions, and, in 1971, developed the classification which is described in this chapter.

At that time only two published summaries of gaming existed. Beale[13] had produced a detailed analysis of the role of gaming. He had distinguished clearly between mental and physical 'games'.

He had observed the distinctions and the similarities between research games and those used for training and educational purposes. He had also seen that there could be similarities of purpose in the use of analytical models, computer simulations, and games, and he had examined the limitations of all three and the ways in which they could complement one another.

In addition, Thomas and McNicholls[14] had carried out a questionnaire study of the value of games played in the United States. They concluded that remarkably little of 'scientific' value had resulted from considerable effort: although learning must have taken place, it could not be made explicit for the benefit of others. They also noted that there was a glamour value in the playing of games on a large scale, and their original purpose, if stated at all, tended to be forgotten.

In 1969–70, a research colleague of the author, John P. Strong, had been studying problems of military information systems and decision-processes. He had proposed a study of the processes of tactical decision-making and planning, in terms of their informational, heuristic and logical content. In a series of games, both the information given to the players about the tactical model used, and the influence that they would be allowed to have on it, were to have been controlled systematically by an experimenter. Although the research programme was never implemented in the form proposed, these ideas have affected the course taken by studies of military information and decision. What is important here is that Strong had looked at various ways in which control over games could be exercised, and he had developed a simple classification. What will now be described is based on Strong's classification, although it has been considerably extended by the author.

The games to be discussed will be representations of the interactions between two systems only. Multiple interactions can be either reduced to this form by aggregating systems, or regarded as being made up from a limited number of two-sided interactions; the second approach will become very complicated even with a small number of interacting systems. The real-world situation is therefore simplified and modelled as involving two players. These are usually representing people or groups of people, although, in certain cases, one side can be played by Nature. There is generally at least one player who is making decisions based on incomplete knowledge; it is the importance of his behaviour, representing that of his real-world counterpart, that leads to the playing of a game.

The description of the structure of a game, figure 4.1, uses the diagrammatic notation previously introduced. The reader is recommended to examine the diagram in order to get some idea of what is involved, and to refer back to it as necessary; the 'classification' labels, in particular, require more explanation (see section 4.3.1). Later, in chapter 5, the diagrammatic notation will be used and extended to aid the discussion of a specific type of game. It may be found that the more general description used here will then become easier to appreciate, even though figure 4.1 includes only what is essential to the derivation of a classification of game structure. It should also be noted that what follows is, in fact, a statement of the logic inherent in the diagram rather than the diagram's being regarded as an illustration supplementing the text.

4.2 The structure of a research game

4.2.1 *The Players*

The players will be called BLUE and RED (a convention widely adopted, and not intended, any longer, to have political significance). BLUE will always represent the real-world actor for whom a satisfactory outcome is sought and who is aligned with the decision-maker on whose behalf the research gaming study is undertaken. The word 'actor' is used of the real-world person whom the player represents, in order to make it clear that there is a sort of game (or play) going on in the real world (this will be referred to again in the penultimate section of this chapter). The players are part of the game and are in control of systems which interact within the game. All interactions in the game have potential effect on *all* systems and subsystems, and these consequences are referred to as *modif*

Consider first the BLUE player. BLU
judgement' is a subsystem of BLUE. It may b

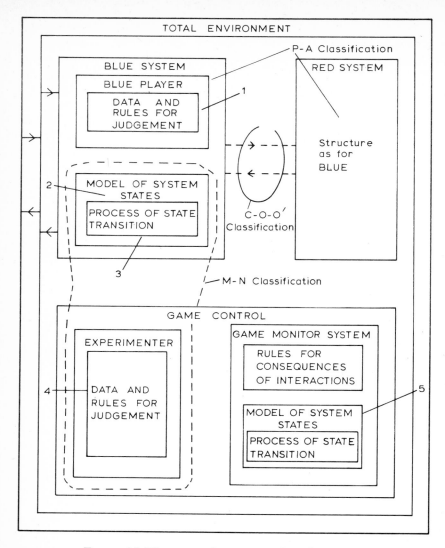

FIGURE 4.1 Diagrammatic representation of a game.

(1) This will include information about interactions and consequences, as provided by the experimenter.
(2) The information about RED is less complete than that about own (BLUE) state.
(3) This is a transition that takes place between system-modifications independent of further decisions by the players.
(4) This includes the purpose of playing the game.
(5) Complete information on the RED and BLUE system states is held here.

of his brain that relates to matters concerning the game. It is modified from time to time through the player (via his sensors) and itself modifies the player and affects his behaviour. But, of course, this 'player' in a game need not be a person. If it is a total automaton (A), it will react in the same deterministic way whenever the same situation (data set) is faced, or else it will be programmed to follow a fully determined course of action in time, independently of the situation. Unfortunately, this seems to be the only type of player that can easily be defined for classification purposes. The essence of a *person*, in this context, is that he will not necessarily use fixed decision rules and may be unable to state clearly what his rules are. Unfortunately, on the other hand, a person may often be indistinguishable from a total automaton, although it must be remembered that a decision rule such as 'if X, then Y' may depend on a decision as to whether one is, in fact, faced with X. Certainly a person's processes may not be, within the constraints of a game, as complex as the logical statistical rules that could be programmed into a computer. Further, such a set of rules might often represent the real-world player better than would a person playing a not fully familiar role. Thus, although the way in which a person reacts to patterns of information is an important distinction between him and an automaton, it is neither easy to state nor easy to measure. All players, not only human beings, capable of reacting differently at different times to the same pattern of information will be regarded as person-like (P).

RED is, of course, seen in similar terms. The decision sets that each player has to manipulate have now to be considered. They relate to the purpose, structure and control of the game.

4.2.2 *The* BLUE *and* RED *Systems*

Both players are subsystems of the systems they control. In the game, BLUE controls an explicit model of systems and their states. It represents the BLUE and RED systems and their environment, or such parts of these as simulated sensors or the nature of the game have enabled BLUE to have knowledge of. This explicit model modifies the total BLUE system and thereby the BLUE player, who in turn may be able to modify his own system and consequently the model. In this loop process, the BLUE player's data and rules for judgement may also be modified. A process, which will be referred to as a process of state transition, will continue until modified by BLUE's decision: simple examples would be a movement of a vehicle on a given course at a given speed during a war game, a steady spending rate during a business game, or a continuation of peace talks during a political or industrial game.

4.2.3 *Game Control*

In games for fun (such as board games and card games), RED and BLUE often share a common physical model, although different parts of the model may be seen by each. The game is controlled (assuming no cheating or arguing) by rules, understood and accepted by each player, which govern the consequences of specified defined inter-actions. For research purposes, this is an inadequate form of game. The researcher must play a major role as an experimenter; he is certainly responsible for the rules, but he must also control the game. He is often referred to as the 'game controller', although, of course, there is a great deal more to be done than is implied by 'control'. For instance, the game has to be designed for a stated purpose; suitable BLUE and RED players must be chosen; and, if it is so wished, constraints have to be placed on the ways in which players may modify their system states and on the rules that govern the process of state transition. It will be suggested, in chapter 5, that 'the researcher' should ideally be more than one person. Further, the players' and the experimenter's rules for judgement, the prevailing rules governing the process of state transition, and the rules governing the consequences of RED/BLUE interactions, must be clearly distinguished from one another.

As far as the game-control system is concerned, the main subsystems are the experimenter, which may be a team and which contains, like the players, a subsystem of data and rules for judgement; and the game monitor system which has, as subsystems, the rules for consequences of interactions and a model of current system states. The last of these is similar to the models in the BLUE and RED systems, but contains a complete representation of the simulated real-world state of the situation being considered.

4.2.4 *The Role of the Experimenter*

The task of the experimenter in deciding on the type of game to be played, on the set of decision processes that he wishes to include in the game (and how he wishes to include these), and on the relative importances of these decision-processes to the purpose in playing the game, is best left for discussion until the classification has been proposed and the range of possible games can be considered. It is, however, necessary, at this stage, to consider one major function of the experimenter: that of deciding whether feasible state modifications (changes to the continuing process of state transition) which may be proposed by the players are in fact to be allowed in the particular game being played.

The experimenter could, if he wished, allow all feasible and desired modifications to be made. In this case, he would mainly be watching the on-going process to be sure that nothing strange occurred that might indicate flaws in the game. This might be something apparently wrong with, or undesirable in, the rules controlling either state transitions or consequences of interactions; or something unexpected in the behaviour of BLUE or RED; or some irrelevant influence on the game either from inside or outside that should have been guarded against. He would also, of course, be ensuring that any consequence or interaction that would provide BLUE or RED with information was suitably interpreted back to them. He would be free at any time to impose delays and distortions on this information, and also to override any automatic rule procedures, so as to avoid or produce any critical situations that might be necessary to his purpose.

It should, however, normally be the experimenter's wish to have the right to allow or disallow modifications. If he cannot exert this right when necessary, then he loses control of the game for the purpose of the experiment. However, the only type of game that seems to be clearly distinguishable by any defined measurement of this activity is a game in which the experimenter refuses to allow state modifications at all. This does not imply a static situation, since there will be a defined process of state transition going on. The player, however, is limited to recording such decisions for state modification as he would have made, given the freedom to do so.

As with the automaton/person-like (A–P) distinction, this is a classification which states either that facilities do not exist, or that they exist in some measure. By the (A–P) classification, either the player has no decision-making facility at all or he has some, however slight. In the case of the experimenter's control of the game, he either allows the player no freedom of decision to modify his system (N), or allows him some freedom to modify (M), however slight. It will be seen later that the initial decision of the experimenter to choose between the A and P, and N and M, modes for his game is conditioned both by the decision sets in which he is interested and by the degree of complexity of behaviour, and consequent analysis, that he is prepared to face.

It is essential, in so far as the experimenter decides to interfere with the freedom of the players, that he should do so in a clear and objective manner. He must consider carefully how much to tell the players about the purpose of the game and about the way in which he will, or may, constrain their decisions, since this may affect their attitudes to their roles in the game and their subsequent behaviour. The experimenter must recognise that he is acting on more complete information than they are, and also that he can never fully realise what the motivations for his human players' decisions are, even if they try to tell him. He must also accept the limitation that he is only human and that he may, inadvertently, become involved as an additional player. He must certainly not use himself as a player in a game which he controls. It is a question of detachment and purpose. An experimenter cannot completely avoid interfering with his experiment, but to the extent that he minimises his influence as a subjective element, he becomes a better experimenter, and more useful results will accrue.

4.2.5 *The Game Monitor System*

There is one final thing to be said about the game monitor system. The experimenter, responding to the players, makes appropriate modifications to his model, and consequences, involving further modifications to his model or to the BLUE and RED systems, are extracted by a logical process involving the rules for interactions.

Once the game is in progress, the experimenter will not usually change these rules. He may, however, have to do so on occasion. This would involve not only modifications to the rules, but possible consequent modifications to the game monitor system, in the sense, for example, that the process of interpretation of rules might become more or less complex and time-consuming.

4.2.6 BLUE/RED *System Interactions*

Unlike the real-world systems being modelled, BLUE and RED interact, in general, only through the game control. The extent to which the experimenter relaxes his control over this interaction is proposed as a further stage of classification. If the physical state of RED is fully known to BLUE, the state of the game for BLUE is said to be open (O); while if BLUE knows only those aspects of RED that are indicated by the interactions that take place in the game (and by external intelligence represented by the experimenter), the state of the game for BLUE is said to be closed (C). Total closure of a game (except to an automaton which merely represents an on-going process) is irrelevant to the experimenter's purpose, since no sensible decision-making could then take place. The extent to which the rules for the consequences of interactions are known by the player is not necessarily determined by whether the game is open or closed to him, although in an open game the rules are more likely to be known. Certainly in an open game, the potential for the other player to modify his state will be known, although his thinking will not be known. A player's aims, policies and interpretations of the data available to him are some of the aspects of his thinking that will be considered, in chapter 5, in a more detailed analysis of the nature of a game.

If, in addition to having full information on RED's state, BLUE is provided with all RED's strategic and tactical thinking, then there is a new level of openness (O') extending to both physical and mental states. The condition where minds are closed, apart from what can be inferred from observed or reported behaviour, is natural to most situations for which a gaming representation is used. A partial openness of mind can be introduced by the experimenter or allowed (with overtones of uncertainty) as part of the communication between the two sides; this is clearly essential for gaming certain business and diplomatic situations. But the complete O' mode of play is an artificial construct that may be deliberately introduced to enable the experimenter to guide the players towards more relevant joint behaviours in relation to the purpose of the game.

A fully open mental state with a partly closed physical state does not seem to be a worth-while combination to include in a classification of games, although it will later (chapter 6) be seen to have some importance in a game-theoretic context. Accordingly, the experimenter, in choosing the type of game to be played, is assumed to be restricted to a separate C–O–O' choice for each of his two players. In figure 4.1, the area to which this aspect of classification refers is indicated by hatched modification lines between the BLUE and RED systems, although this modification normally takes place indirectly through game control. It is implied that more direct modification of BLUE by RED, and vice versa, may take place, if the experimenter so decides, as part of the game structure.

4.2.7 *The Game as a Whole*

Three main systems that are subsystems of the game as a whole have been discussed. There may be other subsystems not defined here. If any are defined in an extension of this work, it is essential to realise that this may introduce new relationships into the description of the game as a whole and that, consequently, the present sub-systems may have to be described in more detail.

It is worth noting that if the game structure is imperfect, un-wanted modifications can occur. In particular, BLUE/RED interaction may take place other than through the game control. In an electrical analogy, the path from the BLUE system out to the game and in-wards from the game to the RED system must provide a high resistance in controlled games.

The game itself lies within the total environment which includes everything that is not the game. Ideally, the game, once in progress, should, like a legal trial, be isolated until complete. In practice this cannot be so: experimenter and players, if human, are frequently moving between the model world of the game and the real world outside. Consequently, unless discipline is imposed, things will creep into the game which should not be there. Modification lines between the game and the total environment are shown by which such effects could take place (figure 4.1).

Finally, this total environment in which the game as a system operates must not be confused with the model situation (environment) in which the game as a model process is assumed to be taking place. The game situation is created partly by the rules for consequences of interactions (between BLUE and RED, and also between BLUE or RED or both and the game environment), and partly by what the players are 'given' at the outset of the game.

4.3 The classification system

4.3.1 *Notation*

To recapitulate, the following notation is used.

B = BLUE player, who represents Us.
R = RED player, who represents Them or Nature.

A = Total automaton (no decision-making capability).
P = Person-like (some decision-making capability).

N = No modifications of system allowed.
M = Some modifications of system allowed.

C = Partial closure of the game, that is a limitation on data about the other player and his system.
O = Open physical state of opposing player and his system.
O' = Fully open mental and physical states of opposing player and system.

A game classified, for example, as B (P; M; C) · R (P; M; C) would describe a two-person game of the type widely played for military, political and business purposes. Usually it is played by

D

human beings, with or without some computerised decision-making[15–17].

Such a game represents, potentially, an upper level of complexity in organisation and analysis (although there are some peculiar difficulties with games in the O′ mode—see sections 4.4.5 and 4.4.6). At the other end of the scale, we have a classification such as B (A; N; C) · R (A; N; C). This is a fully deterministic process as far as decisions are concerned, with none of the attributes normally associated with a game. It may be regarded as a mathematical model, a degenerate form of game. It is, however, of considerable importance because, as Beale[13] says, though perhaps a little optimistically, 'one will nearly always start with an analytical study of a highly simplified model of the problem'.

Such degenerate games may also be included within more complex games to accommodate decision-processes that are considered to be fairly automatic and not of great concern to the experimenter.

4.3.2 *Some Comments on Automata*

An automaton, which is not permitted to modify its system but which may have within it a defined state transition process, is to all intents and purposes ignorant of the state of the opposing system. The appropriate classification is therefore (A; N; C). No useful meaning attaches to (A; N; O or O′): any observations of the opposing system states, and interventions at times when continuation of a state transition appears to be undesirable, will be carried out by the experimenter. If an automaton is designed to modify the system, it must, by definition, carry out modifications in a predetermined manner. It can make no decisions of its own. It must be provided with information about the opposing system and with suitable rules for action. The information on which it operates may be a full or partial description of the state of the other system, fed to it in accordance with further rules, either stochastic or deterministic. Useful automaton games seem more likely to be (A; M; O or O′) than (A; M; C). Because of the extra complexity in choosing information to feed to the automaton, in the closed game, it would only be a small step to allow some decision choice as well; the player then changes status and the game becomes (P; M; C).

4.3.3 *Extensions of the Classification System*

Before discussing more fully the range of games that can be played, it will be useful to consider the possibilities for extending the descriptive power of the classification system. This will be done in relation to each of the four aspects of classification listed in the preceding section.

The extent to which the state of RED is closed to BLUE depends largely on

(1) the structure of the game to meet the defined purpose of the experimenter;
(2) BLUE's facilities for obtaining information and how he uses them; and
(3) BLUE's skill in interpreting and predicting RED's behaviour,

but not all of these aspects are fully covered by the concept of closure, nor are they related solely to that concept. In relation to the situation being gamed, the experimenter may have decided that he only wishes to play decisions that belong to a defined set. This may limit the facilities and skills which BLUE can use. Such a restriction is more properly related to the nature of the players, who are being constrained to carry out less than elaborate decision-making; both the number of classes of decision and the sets of admissible decisions within those classes may have been reduced. This then is a possible qualification of the player classifications B and R.

The qualification of M is more difficult since the extent to which a player is allowed to modify his own system is controlled by the experimenter to ensure that the game proceeds in a useful direction. However, within the limits already imposed by the experimenter as discussed in the preceding paragraph, it may be possible for him to decide whether he is likely to give his players a free hand to modify as they wish, or whether he is likely to be more interested in restricting them to particular modifications or even, perhaps, just noting their wishes to modify, while letting the current process of state transition continue. This last procedure would lead to an N classification.

Finally, we come to the most difficult case, that of qualifying P. How person-like is the player under the limitations imposed by the game structure and purpose? At one end of the scale, it is possible to have a restricted game in which a computer-controlled decision-process can perform as well as, or indeed better than, a human being. At the other end, such a process cannot (yet) simulate the complex data-processing and decision-making of the human being; although this must not necessarily be taken to mean that the simulated behaviour would yield a less satisfactory game, the purpose of the game will often be to examine situations in which human decision-making is an important factor and must be simulated whether it is satisfactory or not. To some extent, the experimenter will then have decided, perhaps on the basis of earlier games, whether his players' limitations provide an adequate simulation. The descriptions he can provide to qualify 'person-like', for the purpose of the game, depend on

(1) his prior knowledge of the decision-processes that can occur in the real-world situation;
(2) his prior study of the behavioural pattern of the kind of people involved in the real-world situation; and
(3) his appreciation of how well the decision set being simulated can represent real-world decisions, bearing in mind also the adequacy or otherwise of the simulated situation and environment.

It may well be that a real human being in a game would lend spurious realism to decision-process simulation, and that equally useful results could be obtained by limited person-like computer processes. The descriptive classification of P must be concerned with how far the player, whether human or not, provides a satisfactory representation of decision-processes for the purpose of the game. It should also be stressed that the descriptive classification that might be applied to B and R has nothing to do with the person-like nature of the players, but with the complexity of decision to which their decision-processes will be applied.

It is quite clear from the above that any classification that can be developed will be limited. Nevertheless, even when game classifications which have no meaningful interpretation, or which are obviously useless for any research purpose, are disregarded, there are still about 100 different categories of game left, out of a theoretical 144 ($2 \times 2 \times 3$ conditions for each of two players). Based on the discussions above, all of these can be given additional unstructured qualification. That *all* of the 100 categories that seem possible offer useful games cannot be stated with conviction, but the range of types of game actually played seems to have been unduly limited.

The next section discusses both the games that have been played and those that it seems possible to develop. They will be referred to as 'operational research' games, since they have mainly been used or considered for use by operational researchers. They have all been regarded as research games, but it is suggested, both in section 4.4 and in the discussion that follows, that this description has not always been justified.

4.4. 'Operational research' games

4.4.1 *A Useful Subclassification*

In using the above classification to describe some of the research games that have been played or might be played, it is convenient to start with the simplest, the degenerate game, and to work up through games of increasing realism. As the games become more of a one-to-one representation of real-world situations, they tend, as would be expected, to greater complexity and, in many cases, to less control of the game by the experimenter. For convenience also, the games will be described under the headings of 'no-person', 'one-person' and 'two-person' games (A–A; A–P or P–A; P–P), although these do not otherwise necessarily represent useful subclassifications.

it will be seen, for example, that these subclasses merge into one another in important ways.

4.4.2 *No-person Games*

These are fully automaton games and can be considered as mathematical models. For example, sets of differential/difference equations representing battle and evaluated by analytical or numerical procedures might be

$$B(A; N; C) \cdot R(A; N; C) \text{ or } B(A; M; O) \cdot R(A; M; O).$$

As far as the analyst (experimenter) is concerned, decisions to conduct the battle in a particular way have already been taken, including those decisions that concern reorganisation when certain states are reached. The whole of the decision-process is therefore subsumed into the process of state transition that controls the BLUE and RED systems in the absence of system modification, or is built deterministically into the automaton.

The experimenter can, of course, observe the process and make changes in the sequence of games played, in order to get ideas about the consequences of the various decisions that can be made. In a sense, he is himself playing a

$$B(P; M; O \text{ or } O') \cdot R(P; M; O \text{ or } O') \text{ game or a sequence of}$$

$$B(P; N; O \text{ or } O') \cdot R(P; N; O \text{ or } O') \text{ games.}$$

He might eventually introduce human players to watch the analytical development of the game, and allow them to make certain specified decisions relating to changes in the system that will alter the equations and thereby the state transition processes. The game would then certainly change its character completely and probably become, in the first instance, a fairly simple game of type

$$B(P; M; O) \cdot R(P; M; O).$$

The experimenter may, indeed, play the game himself in any mode, to obtain insight into what useful extensions of a no-person game could be developed, using either computer-simulated or real human decision-processes. He may also, of course, utilise no-person game processes as part of a more complex game. These are the procedures which Beale[13] has referred to, as was stated earlier.

4.4.3 *One-person Closed Games*

Such games are increasingly common and the following three games indicate the types of decision to which they can be applied.

The DOAE Submarine Approach Game[18] presented to a submarine's commanding officer (RED), a partial representation of a (BLUE) surface task group's movement in an environment containing other groups of ships. The different groups of ships are sensed at long range, through various simulated sensors. RED cannot modify his system, although he is asked to comment on the information received and so provide the experimenter with data relevant to RED's reasons for his eventual decision: which target he intends to attack, and when. BLUE behaviour is predetermined, no BLUE decisions are involved, and BLUE has no knowledge of RED other than a general expectation of his presence, manifested in his [BLUE's] pre-planned system deployment and state transitions. The aim of the game is to provide a decision model of the submariner's problem of selecting the correct target (BLUE) and of making this decision soon enough to be able to close and attack. The game is

$$B (A; N; C) \cdot R (P; N; C),$$

and it ends when the single decision by RED is taken, without this decision's being implemented as a system modification. The game was very successful in its original purpose of examining information/ decision/player relationships and it also became a training aid. In all the games played, the player was in fact a Royal Navy submarine commanding officer, but he represented the enemy. The fact that he *was* a Royal Navy officer limited the interpretation of game outputs, since he could not necessarily be said to behave like *Them*. It is a weakness of most games that *They* have to be represented in some way, although knowledge of *Their* characteristic behaviour is one of the basic uncertainties.

This game is of particular interest for several reasons. Firstly, the simple data displayed are marks on a time/bearing plot, with additional indicators of type and quality. This is all that a submarine commander really has to go on, except for his general briefing about activity and conditions in the operational area and about the likely behaviour of the enemy. The physical simulation of his data is therefore a close representation of reality and can be done cheaply (in practice, it was a marked perspex sheet with strips of adhesive tape covering successive time periods). Secondly, it proved possible to identify one variable, some measure of which was essential to the RED decision to attack. This measure governed the probability of making that decision, given certain other types of data. Assuming that these other *types* of data could affect the decision independently, a simple theory was developed, enabling deductions to be made concerning patterns of information not actually tested or observed experimentally. A brief description of this process has been given elsewhere[19], but a full account of the game has yet to be published.

The game scenarios were devised with great care using 'experts' (see chapter 5), who were submarine and anti-submarine warfare officers. The 'action' took place in an 'area' well known to the players from experience gained during naval exercises at sea. Since the simulated data were also based on knowledge gleaned from such exercises (shipping patterns; oceanographic and weather conditions; sound, radio, and radar propagation conditions; false contact probabilities and so on), a sense of reality was given to the players and a confidence in their 'realistic' reactions was given to the experimenters. The extent to which the player is satisfied with his game environment is obviously of great importance. It should be borne in mind that this game is unusual, in that in the real situation, the decision-maker would have a very limited scope for obtaining, displaying and using data. Therefore, apart from the absence of stress, a submarine commander recognises, in the confined format of the game, something very much akin to the confined and limited environment of his underwater operations room. It would not, in general, be wise to expect that circumstances will always offer such a relatively easy matching of operational and game environments.

The Admiralty Research Laboratory (ARL) Anti-Submarine Warfare Game was developed in the period 1965–67. In the fictional situation played, the submarine commanding officer (RED) was closing in on a task group (BLUE) with the aim of penetrating a screen of ships protecting other naval units. He was allowed to modify his system (course, speed, depth, sensors used) on the basis of partial information about BLUE, which he received from a computer in accordance with the rules governing detection. BLUE's pre-planned state transition was performed by the computer, but no BLUE system modifications were made. The purpose of the game was to examine how RED's tactical decisions affected BLUE's situation vis-à-vis RED at the moment when BLUE became aware of RED. The experimenter did not stop the process until RED had completed his penetration of the screen and attacked the protected units, but the game was truncated when post-game analysis indicated that BLUE would have had to modify his system on the basis of his awareness of RED. The game is

$$B (A; N; C) \cdot R (P; M; C).$$

Possible extensions of this process to two-person games are discussed later.

There are some very interesting facets of this game, particularly the nature of the modifications made by RED to the RED state. These, being long-practised and well-understood sequences of decisions, can each be treated as a whole and they *do not*, in the situation played, affect BLUE behaviour. These decision-sequences can therefore be analysed in relation to the ultimate consequence for BLUE in a way that would not be possible if the separate decisions could not be seen as a whole or if interaction between BLUE and RED took place. A second feature of interest is the idea of 'terminating' the game during the analysis process. Those who seek to obtain more details of the way in which these, or any other aspects, of the game were handled, should consult Mrs B. Kitz, now Superintendent Computer Services, DOAE, who was both one of the designers and one of the experimenters for this game. No written account of the game is freely available, and it was never developed beyond the experimental stage.

The National Coal Board (NCB) Colliery Game[20] is a game in which a colliery manager (BLUE) plays against Nature (RED). BLUE has a plan to cut into a possible coal-productive region on the basis of information from bore holes and past workings in other coal seams. RED, the local geology, is prepared by the experimenter, with the help of a geologist 'expert', in the form of a geological map. As the mine-working proceeds, the manager gets further feedback of information. He has to decide how and whether to modify his plan, including a possible decision to cease operating. The operation is fully costed. The game is

$$B (P; M; C) \cdot R (A; N; C).$$

This game has been of use to colliery managers who, by repeated trials with different Nature states, can test the robustness of their plans. The circumstances leading to any shortfall in coal-production can be identified, and so the real-world plans modified, if possible. The *procedure* of setting up several such games can itself be looked at as a game (see section 4.4.6), although in this case it is a 'game' in the real world, with the actual actor or actors playing their proper roles.

There are strong similarities between the three games described above, although the first is obviously the simplest, because it deals with a single decision. Another game of similar type to the last two has been played in the Police Department of the Home Office.[21] There is no doubt that one-person closed games can be of great value for studying specific limited decision-processes and for providing statistical decision-models for use within more complicated models of wider-ranging operations. They also can provide useful training aids of an explicit (teaching) rather than a subjective (learning) type, and may be developed, largely as computer simulation models, for examining the pros and cons of different organizations or tactics.

4.4.4 *One-person Open Games*

The experimental phase of developing and setting up a game is in itself a game. For example, the development of the DOAE Submarine Approach Game involved 'games' of type

$$B (A; N; C) \cdot R (P; N; O),$$

although they were not recognized as such at the time. It may be observed that a distinction between O and O′ in this context is not very meaningful.

A similar process of game development has been proposed by J. P. Strong in the context of an Army information/decision game. In this latter case, test games were proposed to present a BLUE commander with a developing build-up against which he would have to plan deployments and potential counteraction. He would not initially be allowed to modify his system but only to plan ahead. His system state would be assumed closed to the RED automaton, although the state of RED would, initially, be open to BLUE. Games of type

$$B\,(P;\,N;\,O') \cdot R\,(A;\,N;\,C) \text{ and } B\,(P;\,N;\,O) \cdot R\,(A;\,N;\,C)$$

would be played to develop the automaton, the recording techniques and the experimental control procedures, and to acclimatise the BLUE commanders to the game. The next stage would be to play

$$B\,(P;\,N;\,C) \cdot R\,(A;\,N;\,C)$$

games, followed by games of type

$$B\,(P;\,M;\,O) \cdot R\,(A;\,N;\,C) \text{ and } B\,(P;\,M;\,C) \cdot R\,(A;\,N;\,C).$$

These changes would give information about how commanders are limited by reductions in information and how they might seek to remove this limitation. The permitted modifications would be restricted, in general, to systems for acquiring information and to communication systems.

Mutual manoeuvring or actual combat study would require further extension of the nature of the game. For example, it might require the experimenter's allowing changes in RED's system, in some limited way, based on a knowledge of what BLUE was doing and even of why he was doing it. This means a trend towards a game of type

$$B\,(P;\,M;\,C) \cdot R\,(A;\,M;\,O \text{ or } O').$$

So far, the Army games which have been played in this context have been similar to, and indeed have learnt from, the DOAE

Submarine Approach Game. The main difference between this and the Army games is that, in these, RED rather than BLUE has been played as an automaton (that is B (P; N; C) · R (A; N; C)). Other differences are apparent because of the more complicated information structure; because the game environment is not so 'real'; and because, for example, the single decision (to redeploy) has been replaced by sequential decisions (of partial redeployment). Although these decisions provide no BLUE/RED interactions, they do affect the scope for later decisions. However, from the analyst's point of view it still seems reasonable to classify such a game as N for BLUE since the separate decisions are, in practice, analysed as a whole, and do not affect RED during the game.

There is as yet no written paper on these Army games which can be made available, but some information can be provided by Mr D. W. Daniel of DOAE who has been responsible for their development. The likelihood of any form of open games eventually resulting from these as a step towards a more elaborate closed game cannot reasonably be assessed at present.

Indeed, only one one-person open game is known to have been fully developed and played. *The Wessex Ward Management Game* is essentially a game against Nature (represented by the hospital ward's physical and staff resources, and the patients' behaviour). In different forms, it has been used for teaching, for learning and as a research game. The players have a plan of the nursing unit, and data cards giving information on each patient such as age, diagnosis, the consultant concerned, and whether and when an operation is needed. Other information relates to the needs for nursing and to the nursing workload. Events include the admission or discharge of patients, operations, decisions to move patients within the ward, and so on. The game provides insights into the BLUE policies that must be adopted for the moving of patients within the ward, bearing in mind that the best interests of patients, nursing staff and consultants must all be considered. Further, the game examines the information that may be needed and how different information patterns may help or inhibit the taking of adequate decisions.

It is essentially a B (P; M; O) · R (A; N; C) game, with perhaps some aspects of R (A; M; O), the R classification depending on the detail in which the patient is represented. If BLUE's state is open to RED, whose likely responses to tactics by BLUE are understood and can be statistically pre-planned, it is being assumed that such responses will occur. The Wessex game has, in part, similar objectives to those of the Army information/decision games which have just been discussed. The movement of patients can be regarded as a part of the ward process of organizing information for adequate examination and decision. The openness of the ward in the Wessex game is, however, a characteristic of the real situation and not, as in the Army games, an artificiality such as might be imposed for developing a closed game. The success of the Wessex game, which involves the analysis of sequences of related decisions, was of course dependent on the experimenter's prior degree of understanding of, and ability to define, the general process and its overall aims.

There is fortunately a very full account by Hicks of this game and its analysis[22], including comments which stem from the classification described here. Indeed, the material of chapters 2 and 4, as it appeared in earlier informal documents, was freely used and quoted by Hicks. A useful brief account of this game was provided earlier by the research team of the Wessex Regional Health Authority (see note following reference 22).

Two tentative comments may be made on the selection of one-person games so far described. Firstly, it seems likely that useful ideas for the development of a one-person game may be obtained from similarly classified games regardless of the very different environment that may be involved, more so perhaps than from a game in the same environment but of different type. Secondly, there appears to be a logical progression through one-person gaming that, ultimately, could extend to two-person games. This point will be enlarged on later through analogy with a child's progress through games for fun (chapter 6).

4.4.5 *Two-person Games*

The traditional war game[15–17], with two military commands represented by human players, and the experimenter monitoring the game with full access to the states, plans and, perhaps, intentions of both, is, as has already been mentioned, a game of type

$$B (P; M; C) \cdot R (P; M; C).$$

A wide range of games of this type have been played, including business games and political games, and it might be of value to examine all of these in more detail along the lines of an extended classification, as discussed in section 4.3.3, even though games of so complex a nature do not seem to have proved very useful for scientific purposes[14]. Their use as training aids (learning games) should certainly be considered with care, since they can provide a very realistic environment, enriched by all the complications that, for research purposes, inhibit control and analysis. Other types of two-person games may, however, have much greater research potential, although they are less 'real', and it is on these that discussion will be concentrated.

For example, an obvious variant of the above type of closed game is for each player to play with the full knowledge of the other's physical state (requested modifications of state would then have to be carefully considered by the experimenter to ensure compatibility with the aim of the game). Such a game would be a $B (P; M; O) \cdot R (P; M; O)$ game. Games of this type have often been played, although they have not always been clearly formulated or played for a defined purpose. Such games have been used primarily, at a highly aggregated level, as a subjective check on the outputs of computer simulation and analytical models. This is a very proper operational research use, being part of the extremely difficult 'validation' process for such models. The intermediate game, with one person only playing 'open', viz

$$B (P; M; O) \cdot R (P; M; C),$$

could be a second stage game used for training people to play a closed game, or a game used in conjunction with the doubly open game, for determining the extent to which a player's insight into his opponent's plans is affected by his building up knowledge of the opponent's attitude, and by his lack of information about what actual changes of state are taking place.

A very special extension of the war game, the fully open war game, has been played by RAND under the name of the 'seminar' war game[16]. It classifies as

$$B\,(P;\,M;\,O') \cdot R\,(P;\,M;\,O'),$$

and is played by one group, discussing jointly the plans of the two sides and what they might or might not do. The modifications they make are on the assumption that the real-world systems are closed to one another, so that they have to divorce their judgement from their knowledge and consider how the game might look in closed form and what assumptions and deductions might follow. The experimenter has to be the guiding spirit of the group and decide which of the many avenues opened up are worth exploration. No details of the games played are available because of the sensitive political/domestic nature of the results that were obtained. Such fully open games are not easy to play, and they require qualities in the players similar to those of the experimenter. They should not be played by people who have not had experience of simpler types of game. Although a C 'game' is more common in real life, it is harder to play than an O game, simply because lack of information adds to the number of possible situations and consequences of action that have to be considered. Logically, an O' game might be expected to be simpler than either. However, this seems not to be so, both because such openness of mental states (co-operation) is unfamiliar, and largely unreal, in a competitive situation, and because it forces attention, at any stage, on a far larger set of paired strategies than would generally be considered. As implied above, another disadvantage of an O' game is that players can have difficulty in deciding what they might have done had they not known so much, but there are several compensating advantages—for example, the speed with which variants can be played through, the control over the choice between these variants and over the progress of the game in general, and the avoidance of conflict between the experimenter and his players.

Two-person games, in which modification of system is not allowed (to RED or BLUE or both), may be useful for simulating a rigid or committed 'enemy'. They may also have some value in helping to improve one-person games, and later for developing more general two-person closed games. No such games seem to have been played, so how they might be used is speculative. The introduction of a BLUE person into the ARL game (section 4.4.3), to make it

$$B\ (P;\ N;\ C)\ \cdot\ R\ (P;\ M;\ C),$$

could, for example, extend the game to test the speed of reaction of BLUE to the position created by RED and would so continue the development of the battle situation; it is assumed, in this example, that BLUE would be free to make any decision to change his state, and the game would then end. In an Army game sequence of the type discussed in section 4.4.4, a

$$B\ (P;\ M;\ C)\ \cdot\ R\ (P;\ N;\ C)$$

game would be possible. RED could be limited to deciding when, in the light of BLUE's reaction to otherwise predetermined RED moves, the game should be stopped because of a need to change RED's system (even if RED is a rigid and committed enemy). Once again, open games could profitably be used to obtain experience and develop better closed games.

4.4.6 *The OR Process seen as a Game*

The possibility of regarding real-world situations as games has already been mentioned. In an exchange of views during the preparation of this monograph, Rachel Bodle suggested that the procedure of setting up the NCB Planning Game (section 4.4.3) to test a colliery manager's plans could be regarded as a game against Nature. In this *secondary* game, the analyst as game-maker would be choosing the means of administering and controlling the *primary* game, without knowing in advance which of a large number of possible geological states of Nature would be used. In other words, the analyst would plan the primary game for purposes not defined in terms of the 'scenario'.

The secondary game would have the classification

$$B\ (P;\ M;\ C)\ \cdot\ R(A;\ N;\ C),$$

where BLUE is the game-making analyst and RED is Nature. Although still including the geological state, Nature here is a somewhat different concept from Nature in the primary game. Also, in the primary game, the colliery manager, like the analyst in the secondary game, faces an automaton opponent; in fact the two games have the same classification. In the secondary game, regarding RED as an opponent implies that the analyst's secondary decision could be affected by the fact that the exact 'scenario' (state of Nature) would not be known to him.

If the analyst were allowed to choose the geological state of Nature, in the light of the colliery manager's plans, both games would be differently classified. The primary game could now serve the purpose of testing the manager's responses to selected kinds of situations. At least at the outset of this new primary game, Nature would react in a person-like way to the colliery manager's plans. Such a primary game could be described as

$$B\ (P;\ M;\ C) \cdot R\ (P;\ M;\ O).$$

In this game, the analyst would, in effect, be playing RED in a way which could enable him to influence what kind of interactions occurred. Clearly, in this game, and in games of similar type, there is considerable scope for the invention of a malevolent Nature; the analyst as experimenter will need carefully considered rules to avoid the difficulties discussed in section 4.2.4.

The secondary game, when the state of Nature is chosen in the above manner, poses some difficulty in classification. It seems that there are many ways in which 'the analyst' (who of course is not necessarily one person) may be perceived. Is he still playing Nature, or is Nature a very limited automaton which merely acquiesces in his choice of geology? If the analyst is playing Nature, is he a single person (or undivided group) with the roles of BLUE and RED (as well as being an impartial game-maker); or is he a group in which the BLUE experimental setting-up and the RED geological choice are divided between different but co-operating people? It seems that if Nature is not seen as being really played, the game degenerates into a non-game, but that, in the other cases, albeit in rather different ways, a fully open (O') game is being played.

The same sort of things will be seen to happen in the context of the operational research process itself. It is this process, seen as a game, that will now be discussed.

The ideal interaction between operational analyst and decision-maker can be regarded as a game of type

$$B (P; M; O') \cdot R (P; M; O'),$$

BLUE being the decision-maker and RED the analyst. They are involved in a completely co-operative game seeking the best way to proceed in the decision-maker's interests. There is communication in the fullest sense. This is, of course, not the same game as the one that might be used to represent the decision-maker's primary problem. BLUE and RED have a relationship akin to that of two people getting together to explore and analyse the ways in which a situation might develop. As has already been implied in relation to the 'seminar' game, this activity requires great insight and mental discipline.

In practice, the two players will not necessarily have decided to be fully co-operative. Both have a stake in the game. They may, for example, want their own ideas to be 'right', to see the outcome of the game as a victory for them; the game then becomes distorted. If information, but not purposes, is fully exchanged, the game moves to an O mode, while if some information is not disclosed, by either player, the game moves at least partly into a C mode. Further, certain approaches may be unacceptable to either of the analyst and decision-maker and not properly discussed. Natural caution, prejudice and lack of ability are among the reasons that may make the game less than perfect in the M mode: not *all* feasible modifications will be possible in the situation as jointly perceived.

The game may distort further as players move away from a nominally co-operative stance to the perception of each other as opponents ('us' and 'them'). Intolerance may creep in. Alternatively, one or the other may become unnecessary, the analyst reacting in ways that satisfy the decision-maker's preconceptions and becoming a rubber stamp, or the decision-maker simply acting by rote in accordance with the analysis provided. In such cases there is no real interaction, no conflict, and no game. (This is not the same situation as would occur if, say, the decision-maker played the full role of analyst as well. In such a case he would, with all the difficulties for him that such a double role would involve, be playing a completely open game.)

What seems to happen in part is that analyst and decision-maker have difficulty in playing the co-operative roles that the 'game' demands of them, because they do not expect to share responsibilities, outside the game, with one another. In chapter 5, it will be seen that any conflict game requires a game-maker and an experimenter, but here the analyst and decision-maker are jointly playing these roles as well. An external complication is that professional and personal roles get confused, an effect similar to that discussed in section 4.2.7.

It may be possible, at any point in the relationship between decision-maker and analyst, by examining the secondary decisions that are central to the interaction between them, to find out what kind of game is being played. This may help to identify some of the causes of any conflict between them. It is a use of game classification that may find a role in conflict studies generally, although it must be admitted that this is, at present, mere speculation. The reader may find it useful to return to this argument after reading chapter 5; he should also realise that what has gone before is suggesting a possible important use of the classification, but does not pretend to have explored it very deeply.

4.5 Discussion

This chapter has dealt with many different aspects of the structure of a game, and it will be useful to summarize and to offer tentative conclusions as to the value of the classification proposed. There is a potential ranking of the value of a research game in terms of the difficulty of exercising control, although—unless and until it is possible to introduce some measure of degree of complexity of strategy, in particular—this 'difficulty' will remain too subjective a judgement to give an improved classification. However, it is apparent that a game in which at least one side is an automaton, programmed by the experimenter, should be much easier to control than a two-person game. Further, when the decision complexity is reduced to a single (non-implemented) decision, another step *towards* simplicity of control is made. That everything is *still* far from simple will be the theme of the next chapter.

Another point of interest is the way in which the classification forces the two-automaton, or non-person type of game to be recognized. There is no doubt that, for many operational researchers, such a mathematical model can shed light on some aspects of decision, although decisions are not explicitly included. It is also of value to be able to study the results obtained from simulations which include representations of decision-processes, however simplified or generalised these may be. There is a measure of learning by the experimenter in all game-playing, and by the researcher in all research, otherwise developments for improvement and for follow-up work would not take place. It may be that, at times, a research game has served the researcher as a learning game, and this will be commented on further when management games are briefly treated in chapter 6.

Possible sequences of development of game-playing have been suggested, in section 4.4. These start with simple games and introduce complications gradually. The classification enables this increasing complication to be planned along three separate routes—the involvement of people and the degree to which these people are adequate models of the real-world decision-makers; freedom of decision by the players; and access by the players to information. This will be a subject for further discussion in the next chapter. Later, in section 6.2.5, the need for a planned development of game-playing will be underlined by observations based on the gradual progression from simple to more complex games, which is followed by those who play games for fun.

At least one good research game has been seen to have potential as a teaching game, and even badly controlled games have had learning uses. These links were suggested in chapter 2. Games that are broadly similar are identified by the classification of structure which also identifies some of their important dissimilarities. It would be instructive to classify all operational research models that include decision-processes, and seek hidden similarities in the hope that lessons from one area will illuminate and lighten the tasks in other areas. Some time ago, the author had the interesting experience of generalizing a proposed piece of research on direction-finder development (not itself a game, but similar in some respects) in order to advise on whether there were areas of relevant experience in other fields. The generalised statement gave a lead to a military fire-control study, since it was interpreted as referring to this by another researcher. The two pieces of research were found to be conceptually similar, although the language and detail in which they would normally have been described were very different. The similarities uncovered by the generalisation were, unfortunately, not strong enough to be of great value, although the scientists concerned were helped to discuss and identify the essential differences through its common language.

It is, however, for a less ambitious purpose that the classification was produced and applied. If the five questions asked at the start of this chapter are re-examined, answers can now be given, although it is accepted that they are still far from complete.

Are there simpler games (than large-scale multiple-decision games) that could help towards the same end? There are certainly simpler games that can be played, but they will address only limited aspects of the total decision-process. These simpler games will have a controlled, research purpose. It is not certain whether, for the more complicated games that have been played, the 'end' has ever been adequately defined. If the total decision-process is examined in a game, some learning may certainly accrue, but there is no evidence of explicit findings that can be said to have been firmly demonstrated.

Can the use of a computer simulation, for a similar purpose, be regarded as a sort of game, and in what ways is it different? There is still trouble with the definition of the purpose, but there is no reason shown by the classification not to regard some simulations, if they contain representations of decision-processes, as games. The main difference is concerned with the experimenter's switch from a research to a learning mode.

Is there any relationship between mathematical models and

games? The classification has identified a degenerate game played by two automata. It is implicit that this models decision-processes, but that these are fully known and can be represented, for example, in mathematical terms. Sometimes, therefore, a deterministic mathematical model may be used to represent, adequately for some purpose, a decision-process which is stereotyped or which is one chosen from a set of plausible decision-processes. More importantly, if a game with human players has produced useful statistical models, these can later be most useful as representations of decisions. If, conversely, a mathematical model is claimed to represent a process which is not, in the real world, fully mechanistic, the analyst should be aware of the fact that this model does in some way reduce human decisions to rules, and that what these rules are should be made explicit. Finally, it may be noted that mathematical models can be used to represent parts of the decision-processes within more elaborate games.

What parameters can be selected to define, usefully, the nature of a game? The parameters of the classification, despite the difficulties of any absolute measurement, enable many types of game to be distinguished which have very different natures, and which can be placed in some sort of order of complexity or difficulty for research purposes. There is still scope for inquiry into how the parameters can be measured more exactly, for measurement is necessary if we are to control the variables of the game more precisely than is allowed by the classification alone.

Does such a definition help to select the right type of game to play? This classification has not been adequately tested as an aid to selection. But in the sense that it suggests that some of the simpler one-person games, which have been successful for defined purposes, may be preferred as research games because they can be controlled, it gives guidance for the choice of a research game.

These answers may not satisfy the reader. The arguments leading to them may not be convincing enough. He may wish to ask further questions and not find the answers to these here. The simple fact is that games have never been studied very deeply and there is a lot that is not yet known. The classification should help to structure some of the further inquiry that is necessary.

5. The construction of a research game

5.1 Introduction

This chapter reverts to the language and arguments of chapter 3. It is concerned with describing the logical basis for the construction of a research game. The kind of game chosen will be the simplest useful game, as postulated at the end of chapter 3—a B (P; N; C) · R (A; N; C) game in the terminology of chapter 4. It will concentrate on a single decision-point, played through with varying degrees of information and various players. It is assumed that the first game, at least, of any game-playing study of conflict should be of this kind.

The evidence of the last chapter gives ample reason for believing that control *can* be exercised over such a game. It gives little confidence that a more complicated game could, in general, be so controlled. It is possible that the study of a conflict situation might be extended by stringing together a number of such games to cover successive system levels, and then even further perhaps, by putting together successive strings to cover the conflict's progress over time. At either of these points, it might be necessary to accept a loss in realism, and adapt the game to allow decisions which might be taken by different people in real life to be played by a single player. However, this is merely speculation, and, until the simple type of game has been thoroughly tested as a research tool, it would be unwise to attempt anything more difficult.

The material of this chapter and that of chapter 3 has been widely circulated in an earlier, more extensive version[23], and more recently as a supporting paper on methodology to a NATO Conference on the Environmental Assessment of Socio-Economic Systems. It is the latter, less extensive, form on which this chapter is based. It is not being published in the proceedings of the Conference, due to space restrictions.

The notation which was introduced in chapter 3 will be extended. In particular, new forms of arrow will be used for special purposes. Bowen and Smith's[12] original use of double arrows for most modifications to systems, leaving single arrows for modifications to the attitude or information content of purposeful subsystems, has been abandoned. It had always been intended to use this earlier work—a general study of conflict—to analyse the outcomes of game situations in non-numerical terms, seeking only for descriptions of the limitations imposed on decision by the information available to, and the perceptions of, the players.

What is now described is a framework for moving towards this goal. It is a careful analysis of what is going on in the making, playing and control of a game. Definitions are precise and capital letters imply a special use of words, although their meanings do not depart in major ways from the natural language used earlier. The reader who is not yet intending to develop a game may not wish to take in all the detail provided, but it should nevertheless be useful in helping him to realise more clearly the sort of problems that have to be faced.

The account begins with the structure of a game.

5.2 The model

If the participation of people is overlooked, a game can be thought of as a deterministic model with two main subsystems (figure 5.1)— a model of the real world (the *Game-world*), and a set of *Rules*, describing its behaviour as time passes and as the situation develops. The Game-world has one major subsystem, the *Game-situation*, which includes everything in the Game-world which is thought to have any relevant effect on the conflict in progress. Fairly obviously, the Game-situation is the only part of the Game-world which needs to be modelled in detail. The rest need only be recognized as existing. The Game-situation contains a pair of systems which are in conflict with each other—the RED *System* and BLUE *System*. As usual, it is assumed that BLUE is the system on whose behalf the game is taking place, so the decision on which the game is based will generally be one which has to be taken somewhere within the BLUE system. (It is possible that a RED decision might sometimes need to be examined, although this introduces difficulty— see section 4.4.3, the DOAE Submarine Approach Game. It may be observed that, in the present context, RED's decision would be studied only to cast light on some related BLUE decision in another game of primary interest.) The decision considered here will therefore belong to some *Subsystem* of the BLUE System, which may need to be modelled in rather more detail than the rest of the BLUE System. In particular, the Subsystem will be controlled from inside by one of its own subsystems, the *Decision-maker*. This is so called because it represents the apparatus for making the particular decision around which the Game is built.

Within the model, there are two pairs of system interactions which are important, and must be explicitly modelled. These are the conflict itself, between RED and BLUE, and the interaction by which

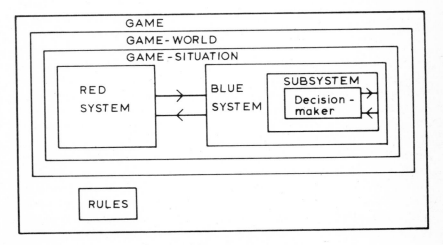

FIGURE 5.1 The model.

the Decision-maker controls, and is affected by, the BLUE Subsystem. In terms of this model, the *decision-point* on which the game focuses can be uniquely defined by the Game-situation as a whole, together with the Decision-maker to which the decision belongs.

5.3 The real situation

The Game-situation of the model just described corresponds to a hypothetical conflict situation which might at some time be reproduced in the real world (figure 5.2). The two situations are essentially very similar; both contain the pair of conflicting RED and BLUE Systems, and, within the BLUE System, a Subsystem responsible for the particular decision that is of interest. Some more details of the interior of the Subsystem have been shown for the real-world situation These are two additional subsystems—the *Receptors*, taking in information which the Decision-maker may need to apply, and the *Effectors*, which act on his decisions. These are not necessarily absent from the modelled subsystem; they are omitted from figure 5.1 only because they are slightly less important in conveying the essentials of the model.

The real difference between the model and the real-life system is that the real Decision-maker *must* be a person (or possibly a number of people). This is crucial to the behaviour of the real Subsystem. Its Decision-maker, being a person, will be essentially unpredictable, in the sense that, in two apparently indistinguishable situations, he may come to two different decisions; and this means that the behaviour of the Subsystem he controls may appear to some extent erratic. Similar effects may result from the presence of any person in any system. Because the presence or absence of persons can be so important, a special notation has been used in these diagrams to distinguish them from non-personal, relatively predictable systems. A person is always represented by a circle, whereas an inanimate system is shown as a box. In fact, in the modelled Game-situation, the Decision-maker is effectively a 'black box', since it is taking the place of a personal Decision-maker who is inscrutable, and whose workings therefore cannot be modelled.

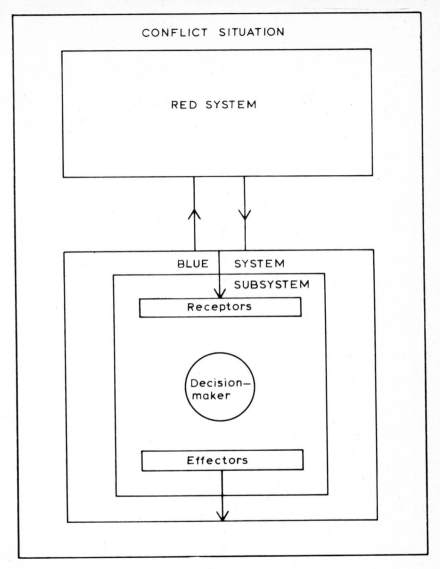

FIGURE 5.2 Real conflict situation.

5.4 People in a game

It is the impossibility of reproducing the real Decision-maker's activities adequately in an inanimate model which makes it necessary to include real people in a game (figure 5.3). The first person who

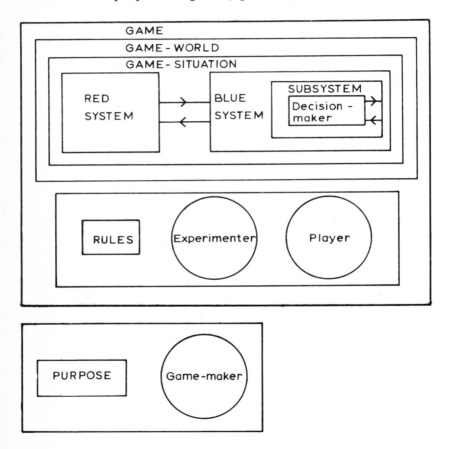

FIGURE 5.3 People in a game.

must be introduced is a *Player*, to animate the modelled Decision-maker; it is assumed that his personal unpredictability can reasonably stand in for that of a real Decision-maker. (In practice, of course, a succession of different players would be used, to correspond to the variety of possible decision-makers in the real world.) As soon as one real person enters the Game, as the Player, it becomes necessary to introduce another, the *Experimenter*, in a kind of administrative role. He is needed, broadly, to communicate with the Player and to respond to his unpredictabilities. His functions will include briefing the Player, passing information to him as required by the playing of the game, and ensuring that he keeps to the rules. He may also offer the cheapest way of keeping the Game-situation up to date, although this activity may be well enough defined not actually to demand the attention of a real person.

The Experimenter, like the Player, is a part of the Game, since it cannot be played without him; but he is not himself a part of the Game-situation, though he may adjust this from outside. He and the Player are both bound by the Rules of the Game, which should govern all the communication required between them, as well as the behaviour of the inanimate part of the model. In fact, the Rules should prescribe the Experimenter's behaviour in all predictable situations so as to curb his own person-like inconsistency, except when this is necessary to respond to that of the Player. The Experimenter, Player and Rules together may be regarded as a 'motor' system for the Game, linked together by their own system boundary.

There is no logical need for any other person within the Game, but the model will necessarily have been constructed by a person outside itself—the *Game-maker*. He must both construct the Game-situation in its original state, and compose the rules which lay down how it develops, so he is eventually responsible for the whole of the inanimate part of the Game. The only components of the Game which he does not create are the Experimenter and the Player, and even they are partly controlled by his Rules. This construction will not take place in a vacuum; the Game-maker must have a *Purpose*, either of his own or dictated to him by someone else. This Purpose will at least specify the kind of information the Game is to generate, and may also suggest the kind of situation to be modelled, or the system level of the decision-point to be chosen. The Game-maker and his Purpose may be regarded as a 'creating' system for the Game, and may also be enclosed within their own system boundary.

5.5 Activities of persons

The presence of people in a game is important because of their unpredictability and, in addition, because they can do two things which non-personal systems cannot: they can, first, act purposefully, both on systems and on other people, and, second, communicate with one another. (They may also be said, in a sense, to receive 'communication' from inanimate systems, when they are able to draw information from these.) Both of these activities provide special opportunities for irregular behaviour and experimental error, so that it is useful to distinguish between these and ordinary, non-person-like interactions (in which persons may also participate). Communication may give special openings for human misunderstanding, so it is also desirable to differentiate between this and other kinds of purposeful action. This is done in subsequent diagrams by adapting the original kind of interaction lines, to show communication by an empty-headed arrow, and purposeful action (not specifically communication) by a solid-headed arrow.

In the Game (figure 5.4), the only communication is between the Experimenter and the Player, and it is regulated by the Rules. It come, in fact, within the 'motor' system. This particular interaction is reciprocated, but this need not automatically have been so, since these arrows depend only on the intentional activity of persons. The Player's manipulation of the Decision-maker system, and the Experimenter's adjustment of the Game-situation as time passes inside the Game, are both purposeful actions with no purposeful reaction, and so is the Game-maker's original construction of the Game. In point of fact, the communication between the Experimenter and Player is also purposeful, but its character as communication is more important. It does not follow that all communication will be purposeful in quite the same sense.

These special arrows can properly be used only in certain

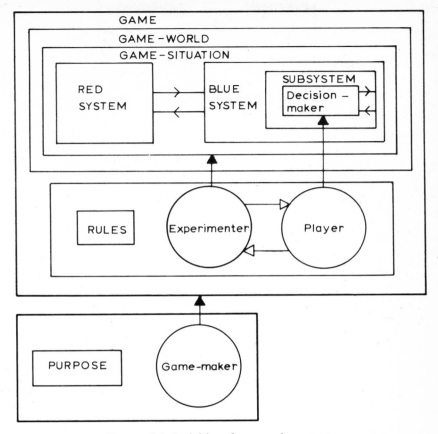

FIGURE 5.4 Activities of persons in a game.

circumstances. They both represent actions characteristic of people, so at least one person must be involved in each such interaction; in diagrammatic terms, each of these arrows must either begin or end at a circle. A solid arrow, for purposeful action, must *begin* at a circle, since only persons can act purposefully; but clearly it can end at any kind of system, since people can act upon things as well as upon other people. An empty arrow, for communication, must *end* at a circle, since only people can accept information, but it may begin at any kind of system from which information can be derived. This is illustrated by the person-like interactions in the real world (figure 5.5), where the Decision-maker, a person, receives one-way communication from the Receptors and then acts purposefully, without reaction, on the Effectors, both of which are inanimate systems. There is, of course, no reason why communication and purposeful action may nct be between *two* people, with a circle at each end of the arrow. In this case the activity is likely to be reciprocal.

It does not follow that unspecialized, 'non-personal' interaction lines must indicate an activity with no element of purpose or communication, or, for that matter, that a nest of box-like systems contains no people. These 'non-personal' notations simply omit to specify whether or not people and their activities are present, whereas the 'special' notations specifically draw attention to them. For example, again in the real world, the main interaction of the conflict between RED and BLUE is shown as non-person-like, and the RED System as containing no persons, only because this diagram is specially drawing attention to a particular part of the interior of the BLUE System; the real RED System will in fact almost certainly contain several persons, and the interaction itself should certainly be purposeful, and is likely to involve communication as well.

5.6 Roles and rules

5.6.1 *Roles in a Game*

The two persons involved in the playing of a game—the Experimenter and Player—will each have to fill more than one role. It is important that these roles should not be confused with one another and allowed to interact in ways that they should not. The roles should correspond to different sections of the Rules covering the Experimenter's and Player's behaviour during the game. Three such sections are shown in figure 5.6, and are described below.

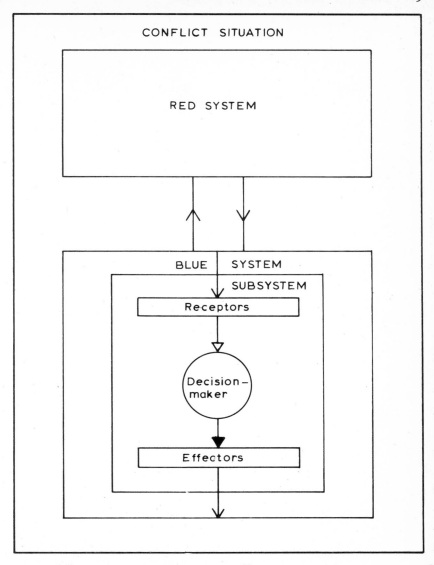

FIGURE 5.5 Activities of persons in a real situation.

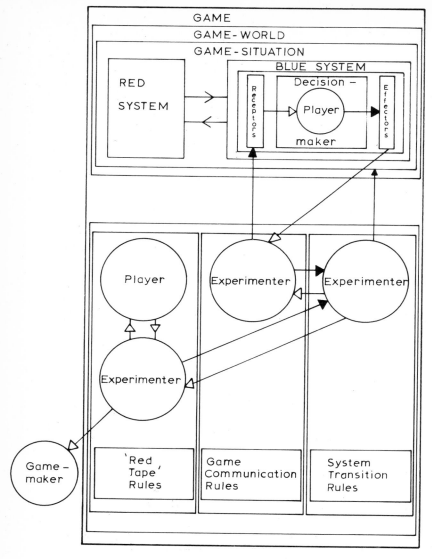

FIGURE 5.6 Role in a game.

The '*Red Tape*' *Rules* cover all the administrative matter of the game—briefing the Player, stopping, starting, and any interruption of the game to cope with unforeseen circumstances. They specially affect the Experimenter in his 'administrative' role, and so control most of the direct communication between the Experimenter and Player as conscious participants in a game. They may also cover any report of the results from playing the Game to the Game-maker, or to any other person who requires them.

The *System Transition Rules* lay down how the Game-situation should change, both with time, and in response to the Player's moves (if any). The Experimenter can have a further role in applying these rules to the Game-situation and bringing it up to date where necessary. This is a relatively mechanical role, and not one that makes specific use of the Experimenter's status as a person. It is one that he is liable to be given because it is more economical to assign it to him than to an additional person or a computer.

The *Game Communication Rules* cover communication within the Game between the Experimenter, and the Player in his essential role as 'Decision-maker' for the BLUE Subsystem. This must be arranged to make the Player's information and options within the game as nearly as possible equivalent to those of a real decision-maker, so that he perceives himself as using the Receptors and Effectors of the BLUE Subsystem. This may be done by the Experimenter's feeding in information in the proper form for the real system which the Game models, and then, after the Player has responded, making appropriate adjustments to the Game-situation in the same way as the real Effectors would (if the game continues so long). In fact, the Experimenter's communication with the Player may be seen as having two stages in each direction. He may be seen, first, as purposefully selecting information for the model Receptors, which then communicate it, in suitable form, to the Player; and then, after the Player's decision is reached, as being informed of it by the model Èffectors, which receive it as a purposeful command from the Player. In practice, however, the whole of this exchange is handled by the Experimenter and the Player between them.

5.6.2 *Interactions between Roles*

Not all of these roles are completely independent. The Player's two roles should ideally be so, and should be kept separate as far as possible, so that, although his explicitly 'playing' role is necessary in order for the game to be explained to him, he is not too much influenced by the idea that he is 'only playing' while he is acting as the 'Decision-maker'. The Experimenter's three roles, however, will all affect one another at least indirectly, both by giving the cues to call other roles into play, and by providing the material for them to work on. In his central role of communicating with the Player as 'Decision-maker', he both passes on the fresh information created by himself in applying the System Transition Rules (communication), and receives responses from the Player which prompt him to make further adjustments to the Game-situation (purposeful action). Again, in his 'administrative' role, the Experimenter may be required to stop, or intervene in, the running of the game, and the data telling him to do this will be supplied by himself in his 'system adjustment' role, which in turn may be affected by the type of intervention required: for example, the Experimenter may have to meet an unforeseen action on the Player's part by freezing the System Transition Rules, and constructing the system's immediate response on his own initiative. The Experimenter's roles as 'administrator' and 'communicator' may impinge on one another in certain circumstances, but this is liable to amount to no more than stopping or suspending game communication through the freezing of the development of the Game-situation, and this can be accounted for indirectly through the suspension of the System Transition Rules.

5.7 Communication

This is discussed specifically because it gives some of the best opportunities for misunderstanding and error, and also because refinement of the rules covering communication between the Experimenter and Player offers some of the most elementary developments which can

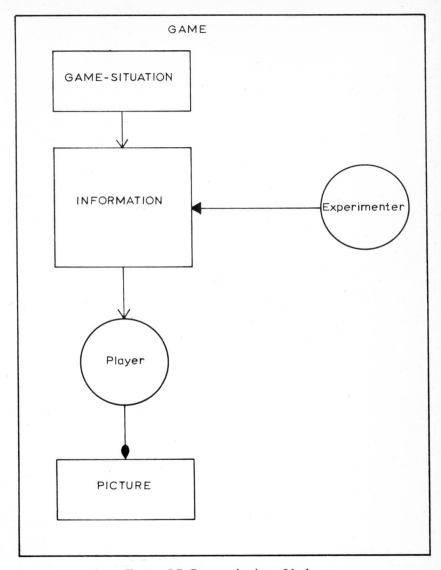

FIGURE 5.7 Communication—Ideal.

be made to a simple game. For this purpose, only communication with the Player in his 'decision-making' role is considered.

In the ideal, simplest case (figure 5.7), the Player will be given access to a body of *Information* which exactly reflects the current state of the Game-situation. This information will be completely determined by the Game-situation, together with a section of the Rules to govern its conversion and passing on to the Player; making this conversion is part of the Experimenter's 'communication' role. It is assumed, in this 'ideal' case, that the Experimenter applies the rules without person-like errors, and so actually produces the Information system implied by the Game-situation. In this simplest game (to describe), the Player will automatically be given all of the existing information about the Game-situation; in terms of the diagram, the Information system as a whole will be acting directly on the Player. He will use this information to construct a *Picture* of the Game-situation, to use in reaching a decision about what he should do, but his picture-building will be person-like, subject to errors and faulty deductions, and so it may result in a distorted picture of the 'real' situation. This particular distortion is not unwanted in the Game—it is part of what the Player is there to supply—but it, and other instances, are important enough to warrant being specially marked. This kind of unpredictable reaction by a person to a stimulus is marked in all cases by an arrowhead with a round base.

The above describes the ideal situation for a game, but since the Experimenter, as well as the Player, is a person, it will not actually occur. The Experimenter, applying the appropriate rules to the Game-situation, will actually produce a different body of information—the information *Possessed by the Player*—to contribute to the Player's construction of his Picture (figure 5.8). The main Information system will now be a hypothetical structure: the system that *would have* been produced if the Experimenter had consistently behaved as the Game-maker intended. The divergence between the ideal and actual information systems may be of several kinds—alteration, omission or simple delay—not all of which are easily included in a simple diagram. If, however, only the last two are considered, the information Possessed by the Player may be assumed

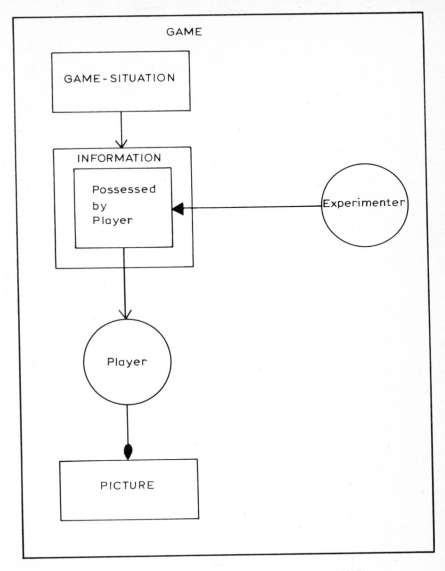

FIGURE 5.8 Communication—Actual.

to be a subsystem of the Information system as a whole. This information Possessed by the Player is purposefully constructed by the Experimenter. He is, of course, working from and almost certainly distorting the matter contained in the Game-situation, but since this last link is not included in the diagram, his construction of the information Possessed by the Player is not indicated by a round-headed arrow. This is because these arrows denote distortion *of* something, and in the diagram nothing is shown for the Experimenter to distort.

As the treatment of communication in a game becomes more complicated to describe, the game as an experiment may become easier to control. This should happen when censorship of the Information system is introduced (figure 5.9). In this case another 'ideal' subsystem, of information that is *Allowed to the Player*, will be defined, and, at least in theory, everything that he is given to know should be taken from inside this system. In fact, in a game without further complications, it should be identical with the information Possessed by the Player, but as before the Experimenter's activity will ensure that this is not the case. He has, indeed, a fresh opportunity for error, since he can now give the Player information which he was never intended to have. (This possibility is not shown in figure 5.9, where the information is shown as a subsystem of that Allowed.)

Another complication may be the first development to be introduced after the simplest possible game has been played. This is the facility for the Player to make specific inquiries about gaps in his knowledge of the Game-situation (figure 5.10), which may provide a quicker way for the Experimenter to learn what kind of information the Player most needs. In this case, the information Possessed by the Player can be divided into two parts—the information he is *Given*, automatically, and the information that must be specifically *Requested*. This last body of information is likely to have important effects on the results of the Game. The Player's Picture of the Game-situation will generally have gaps, and these in turn will have their effect on him, possibly preventing his choosing a course of action with any confidence. This is an ordinary, non-person-like interaction. The Player will then be able to put specific inquiries to the Experimenter, with a view to filling the gaps in the Picture. This is an

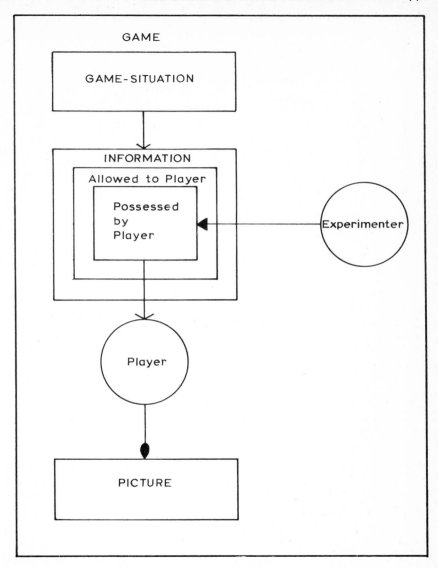

FIGURE 5.9 Communication—Censorship.

instance of communication; but, because the Player may not phrase his questions clearly, or may even choose them wrongly for what he wants to know, it is liable to distortion. It is therefore represented by a rounded arrow. The information Requested by the Player will be cumulatively collected by the Experimenter in response to these inquiries. This is a purposeful action. It also may be distorted, as the Experimenter may misunderstand what is needed and as a result pass on more or less than is really asked for. This distortion has also been indicated in figure 5.10.

These later instances of person-like behaviour are not necessarily desirable in the Game, and some are positively unwanted. Some of the Player's variable behaviour will be useful in simulating real life, but the Experimenter's, as a rule, will only introduce non-uniformity into the experiment. Since the Experimenter is necessarily a person, his inconsistencies cannot be wholly prevented, but it is at least useful to be aware of where they may be introduced. Locating the openings for these inconsistencies is the purpose of figures 5.8–5.10.

5.8 Some directions for further inquiry

5.8.1 *Comments on Purpose*

In the earlier account of the research on conflict games[23], some consideration of the purpose of a Game-maker in constructing a Game was included. It has already been made clear in chapter 2 that classification of games according to purpose is not simple. Indeed, because it tends to be much more subjective than a classification of structure it is likely to be less well defined, and consequently it may often be more difficult to interpret. Nevertheless, it is worth quoting the brief comment which follows, noting that it originally referred specifically to games in the general context of conflict and crisis in an interaction between two purposeful systems. It offers a list of purposes for games, which may be generalisable, and it is of great importance to game design that the purpose should be stated as explicitly as possible. This list in fact covers most of the purposes suggested in section 3.7, but arranges them slightly differently.

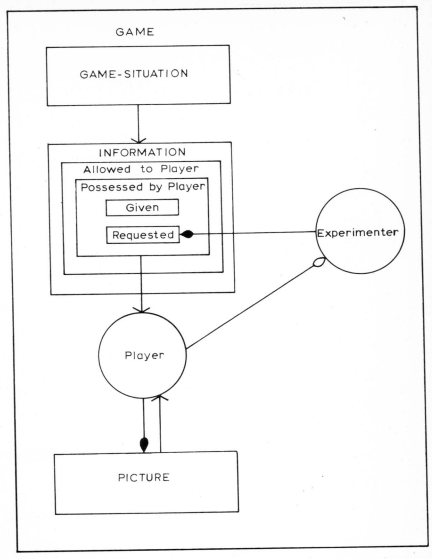

FIGURE 5.10 Communication—Inquiry.

The Game-maker may wish to investigate, in a series of games, some or all of the following:

(1) for a given system,
    (a) the way in which instructions about aim or policy develop as they propagate through the system, and
    (b) the way in which information is transformed during transmission through the system;
(2) for a given level of a system, the aims which are adopted at that level;
(3) for a given decision-point,
    (a) the kind of information and capability needed to prevent crisis, and
    (b) the effect of specified policy constraints on the decision taken; and
(4) for a given decision-point, with given information and policy constraints, the likelihood that various decisions will result.

According to his purpose, the Game-maker would vary different factors. For (1), the main variables would be the Player and the system level. For (3), the main variables would be the Player and the information available to him. For (4), the only variable would be the Player. (2) is a special case which might need a very different sort of game from that which has been considered in this chapter. Indeed, the purposes assumed in developing the above concepts of a game were limited to (1a), (3a), and (3b)—to ways of influencing the outcome of conflict in the light of already specified aims.

5.8.2 *Variables*

The identification and treatment of the main variables in a game is of great importance. In order of the increasing complexity of game that would be needed to incorporate them usefully, the primary variables are the Player; the form and content of what information is passed to the Player; the decision-point (that is, the specific levels of decision, relative to the BLUE system, that a player may be expected to make in the same Game-situation context); and the decision-sequence (that is, the particular chain of decision-points within the BLUE system, resulting from a development in the Game-situation). But also, in any particular game, the definition of these variables may need further (secondary) variables, and these cannot be discussed usefully in a general conceptual way. It is also apparent that what can be said about the primary variables above must be somewhat vague and speculative until practical experience from controlled experiments with games is available.

It is for these reasons that more extended comments on variables are not included here. It is recognized that the study of variables in a game should tend towards the establishment of a theory, rather than being left to ad hoc consideration, game by game. It is also recognized that this direction of study cannot be usefully attempted at the moment.

5.8.3 *Defining the Game-situation*

Another aspect of the original study[23], which was still rather tentative, concerned the possible adaptation of the gaming method to construct the total information set that defines the Game-situation. The Game-maker is likely to need the help of an 'expert' to ensure that the detail of the Game-situation is both plausible and consistent. What, in the context of conflict and crisis, is an 'expert', and how can such a person best be used?

In general, 'experts' are made by experience, and, while an individual can be expert in any general context in which conflicts and crises can develop, he can rarely be expert in *how* they may develop. (Crises by definition are non-routine.) The proper role for an 'expert' is not therefore to design the whole development of the conflict, but to ensure that the content of a scenario does not conflict with the possible reality, so far as that can be known.

The 'content' of a scenario includes both the broad outlines of the fictional conflict's 'history' and development, and detail about specific aspects of the situation at different stages in time. It is possible that both can be defined more efficiently if the Game-maker, either alone or with a fully co-operating Player, plays an informal open (O or O') game. This, by forcing him to face the incomplete decision-situation, will bring the Game-maker's attention to those parts of it which are still missing; the help of an 'expert' can then be used in filling in these gaps convincingly. If, in fact, the co-operating Player is an 'expert', this should be an advantage at both stages of the process.

The expected form of such a 'scenario game' would be as follows. The Player would be presented with a first version of the scenario in the form prescribed by the eventual game (so far as this was yet determined), and asked to make the necessary decision. He would be asked to comment on the adequacy of the scenario in its current state, and his reasons for deciding as he did. The Game would thus be O' for the Game-maker and O for the Player, so far as an incomplete scenario would permit. The scenario would then be altered accordingly and the Player presented with the new version, and so on until the Player was satisfied. The Player would not be required to provide material for the scenario, but merely to check the credibility and completeness of the story presented to him. It may be desirable also to attempt to obtain a reasonably comprehensive list of options for the Decision-maker as well as an explicit estimate of their likely outcomes, but this seems to be a matter for consultation with the same or another 'expert'.

A 'scenario game' would be suited, primarily, to generating 'factual' information about the Game-situation. Since the purpose of a 'scenario game' would be to build up a 'complete' picture of the Game-situation for the Game-maker, the 'expert' would not be restricted to questions bearing directly on the decision of the Game. Nothing would be discarded as irrelevant so that the final picture should contain all the material that *might* be needed, either to be given to the eventual Player, or to enable the results of the game to be assessed. It should contain, at a minimum, all the information that a Player might be expected to find necessary for his decision.

Such an ideal result may not be achievable, but it is believed that it can be approximated to very closely—at least closely enough not to make the Player feel that he is in an unreal situation, and certainly closely enough for the purposes of the Experimenter and the

Game-maker. Such an attempt to construct the scenario for a game is worth trying; it would help to formalise the unstructured process of discussion and debate that would be the alternative.

5.8.4 *General Comment*

What has been discussed in this chapter offers a logical basis for the construction of the simple one-person games that may be played initially, and it gives some guidance for later extension of these. As more elaborate games become possible, an explicit account of how they can and should be controlled will be needed. Unless the logical process of the control of research games is clear, there is a likelihood that past errors will be repeated.

Games have all too often been called research games despite their having no stated purpose nor any coherent method of control in order that any research purpose might be met. Consequently, the emphasis has been on game-playing rather than on game-analysis. Players and those who have constructed games have had fun, much has been learnt by individuals, but, compared with the effort expended, remarkably little of lasting value has been produced.

A better future for games as operational research tools is possible. This will be discussed in chapter 7. The intervening chapter deals briefly with some aspects of games which cannot be altogether omitted, but whose treatment in detail is not sufficiently relevant to this monograph.

6. Games for fun, game theory and management games

6.1 An explanatory note

This chapter considers, briefly, games other than those in general use for research purposes. They are treated primarily in the context of their potential relevance to operational research games or to the research process itself. Reasons for the absence of a more extensive bibliography have already been given in the opening chapter (section 1.5).

It will be seen that the classification developed in chapter 4 enables the structure of games for fun, management games, and the relatively simple experimental games for behavioural research which are associated with game theory, to be categorised. Apart from the comments that can thereby be made on individual games, it is encouraging to find that a classification of structure developed for one purpose can relate to games for many other purposes. Not only does it confirm that the structural properties of research games have not accidentally been confused with their purpose-oriented properties, but it lends support to the view (see figure 2.2) that there are in fact very close relationships between the various primary purposes of games.

Needless to say, this should not be pushed too far. But it is as important to see similarities, when they exist, as to identify real differences. It is important because, otherwise, conceptual ideas from one area are not used in another, since they do not get expressed in a common language—a point already made in relation to research models in general in the final section of chapter 4.

6.2 Board games and card games

6.2.1 *General Comment*

In order to use the classification system of chapter 4 to label the games that children, and adults, play for fun, it is obvious that the concept of the experimenter has to be generalised. Here, all the 'experimenter' is presumed to have done is to set rules for permissible state transitions and to allow moves freely in accordance with these rules. There is, however, no experimenter present unless one of the players is consciously trying to learn from the game, in which case he is in the dangerous position of also being the experimenter; or unless players are being taught the game, in which case their teacher is the experimenter. In this latter case, closed games are initially played as open games which tend to be O'.

Games, as they are defined in this monograph, call solely for mental activity. Sports, on the other hand, require also a physical skill. Horse racing is a sport if you ride the horse and a game if you back it! It is then a game against Nature with complicated rules and information requirements. It would be classified as

$$B (P; M; O) \cdot R (A; M; C).$$

The nature of the automaton is complex, as is the open/closed nature of the RED system. The modifications made by RED are continuous, and BLUE may modify his own state (his bets) up to the moment of the start of the race. RED continues to modify without any interaction with BLUE's behaviour, unless the race is rigged! This is a fairly light-hearted attempt to fit a rather odd game into the pattern presented here.

6.2.2 *Board Games*

Chess is one of the most complex and skilful of board games. Its classification is

$$B (P; M; O) \cdot R (P; M; O).$$

G

There is a subtle variant of Chess called Kriegspiel. This is a three-board game in which the players learn little or nothing of opponents' moves. Only when pieces interact, or moves are not allowed, do they start to gain information from the monitor board. Not surprisingly, the classification is the same as for the three-room 'operational research' war game,

$$B\,(P;\,M;\,C) \cdot R\,(P;\,M;\,C).$$

Again, if one or more people study a Chess game position and try to analyse it to determine the outcome, they play both sides in a

$$B\,(P;\,M;\,O') \cdot R\,(P;\,M;\,O')$$

game; this is a 'seminar' game (section 4.4.5) or even an OR process (section 4.4.6). These last two games cannot be played successfully by players who are not skilled in the normal game of Chess,

$$B\,(P;\,M;\,O) \cdot R\,(P;\,M;\,O).$$

It will also be recognized that very few Chess players fail to go through a considerable cycle of learning with other, simpler games. It is similarly not surprising that the three-room war game has, in at least one case (at DOAE), yielded to a simpler, open type of game, nor is it surprising that the RAND seminar game is found to be of even greater subtlety and difficulty.

There are other board battle-games, such as Naval Tactics and Tri-Tactics, in which, initially, the opposing states are closed. As in Kriegspiel, the states are only slowly discerned as interaction (challenge or avoidance of challenge) takes place. Such games are also

$$B\,(P;\,M;\,C) \cdot R\,(P;\,M;\,C),$$

as is the pencil and paper game of Battleships. Ludo (a board game for 2, 3 or 4 players) is a

$$B\,(P;\,M;\,O) \cdot R\,(P;\,M;\,O)$$

game like Chess. There are two differences in degree. First, there is far less complexity of choice, in Ludo, in the moves that change the state of the system (in both of these games, the state changes in discrete moves; time-varying states between decisions do not occur).

And also, in Ludo, there are constraints placed on allowable moves by the fall of a die; sometimes only one move is possible and, for that move, the player is an automaton (this happens rarely in Chess, mostly towards the end of a game). There is, in fact, very little skill in playing Ludo, but in so far as it is similarly classified, it has a distant kinship with Chess.

A more elaborate game of the same type as Ludo is Sorry!® This has more possible risks and strategies to think about, as well as more moves to choose from when a card, replacing the die, is drawn. There is still a long way to go before Chess is reached, but there is also a very large number of games to provide a near-continuum of variation in the part played by the person and the kind of decisions he takes. Backgammon, Halma, Draughts, and Turkish Draughts are such games of increasing

$$B\,(P\,;\,M\,;\,O)\cdot R\,(P\,;\,M\,;\,O)$$

strategic complexity, and near the top is the Chinese game Go. Whether this is more or less complex than Chess is debatable.

6.2.3 *Degenerate Board Games*

There are two well-known board games in which the players are mere automata, albeit in different ways. (These include games in which the 'board' is just a surface holding the 'pieces' or even a sheet of paper.) The first is Snakes and Ladders, a game of no skill whatsoever, in which the players interact only at the moment of victory. The throw of a die controls the way in which the states of the two systems change; the players respond automatically to the rules that govern moves. The second is Noughts and Crosses, which is degenerate only because the strategies (sequence of moves) are so limited that the sequence of play can be fully pre-programmed. Both may be considered as $B\,(A\,;\,M\,;\,O)\cdot R\,(A\,;\,M\,;\,O)$ games. The former is not of much interest since the openness of the game is irrelevant in the absence of interaction (the rules used by the author, as a child, allowed both pieces to occupy the same square). The latter is of distinct interest since, for immature minds, it is

$$B\,(P\,;\,M\,;\,O)\cdot R\,(P\,;\,M\,;\,O);$$

it therefore holds, in a very limited way, something of the mystery of Chess. It is interesting to note how much more complex Noughts and Crosses becomes when extended to three dimensions. The set of decisions, and whether any one decision leads to win, lose or draw, is no longer easy to define.

A similar situation arises with Nim, a class of game usually played with matches. In the best known Nim game, the moves consist of taking matches from one of a number of separate piles. The winner is the one who takes the last match (or, if one so wishes, the one who does not). A complete theory of such games is possible[24]; anyone skilled in rapid binary arithmetic can win, unless his opponent is equally knowledgeable, in which case the winner is defined by the starting state.

There are other games of the same type, some of which need long analysis before the playing of them becomes a degenerate game. Martin Gardner's mathematical column in *Scientific American* has discussed many such games, which often look much simpler than they are. In learning to understand them one plays

$$B (P; M; O) \cdot R (P; M; O)$$

games until, when one has exhausted the logic of the game, an uninteresting game,

$$B (A; M; O) \cdot R (A; M; O)$$

is all that is left.

There are also one-person puzzle games of the same complex nature; they may involve nothing more than a few plastic or wooden shapes and simple rules, but the variety of choice inherent in the puzzle is surprisingly large. They are definable as

$$B (P; M; O) \cdot R (A; N; C)$$

games, although RED is effectively a system that constrains, but does not respond. Again, one is eventually left with a degenerate game.

6.2.4 *Card Games*

Most card games for two are

$$B (P; M; C) \cdot R (P; M; C)$$

games. Bezique, Canasta, Piquet, German Whist and Jo-Jotte (Josephine Culbertson's two-player variant of Contract Bridge) are of this type. Bridge itself is of the same type, if one interprets a four-person, but two-sided, game as a two-person game. Interestingly, some of the information of one's own (more correctly, one's part-ner's) state is closed, a condition that applies to two-person war games when more than one echelon of command is represented, and the experimenter ensures that the 'fog of war' exists. In Bridge, some information about the partner's cards can be communicated in accordance with the rules of the game. This, however, takes time, and misinterpretations occur, as they do in war.

Closed two-person card games are usually taught by turning them into equivalent

$$B (P; M; O \text{ or } O') \cdot R (P; M; O \text{ or } O')$$

games. There is also an Autobridge teacher game which, although difficult to classify, is basically

$$B (P; M; C) \cdot R (A; M; O').$$

RED is fully pre-planned, and the teacher control eventually forces BLUE to make the correct prescribed moves. Statements are included as to why alternative moves that BLUE might suggest are incorrect.

Many well-known and complex card games are not of concern here since they are essentially many-person games, for example, Poker. At the other end of the scale is a game, well known to children, which is one of the first they learn to play, called Strip-Jack-Naked. It is a degenerate game of no skill whatsoever (cheating excepted!). It is apparently a

$$B (P; M; O) \cdot R (P; M; O)$$

game, as played, although a player has only one permissible move each time, depending on the equally forced move of the other and on the card sequences in the piles of cards held by the players. It is therefore logically

$$B (A; M; O) \cdot R (A; M; O),$$

because, if played by a machine, the result would be the same. It teaches little except the recognition and handling of cards and, in a primitive way, something of card values. It also provides some insight into chance events with a shuffled pack, since the probabilities of the occurrence of court cards are important, even though, in any one game, they are predetermined.

Finally, there are the one-person card games known generically as Patience. There are hundreds of such games that provide a near-continuum from automaton behaviour to considerable mental skill. They are mainly

$$B (P; M; C) \cdot R (A; N; C)$$

games, although the most skilful are

$$B (P; M; O) \cdot R (A; N; C).$$

In these games RED is Nature, the result of a shuffle and deal, unchanging from the moment of starting play. At the lowest end of the scale, again an early card game of childhood, is Clock Patience, in which the moves are automatic; the only (adult) interest is to learn something about chance. Clock Patience can be classified as

$$B (P; M; O) \cdot R (A; N; C),$$

although, as with Strip-Jack-Naked, the BLUE modification is the only move permitted by the rules.

6.2.5 *Relation to Research Games*

There are aspects of the learning process which children go through, that relate to earlier comments (section 4.4) on the range of complexity of possible research games and on the sequences of games through which a final research game might be developed. Children do *not* start with the game of Chess. Although they may start with games that are similarly classified, these games are simpler in terms of strategy choices, even to the point of being, theoretically, degenerate games. They also learn through one-person games of various types, some of which involve quite complicated strategy-sets.

It would be optimistic to believe that experience of playing games for fun enables a person to understand how to construct a game, and the rules of a game, in order to provide explicit information about decision-processes. (It may of course make it easier to act as a player in such a game.) The game-maker therefore needs special experience. It does not seem unreasonable to suggest that this can best be gained by developing games in a similar sequence to that which an unskilled player might demand for learning.

The link between games for fun and research games may be a difficult one to state with any greater precision. However, a game-maker who has played games for fun should have a better understanding of the requirements of his players, and it has already been seen that this is crucial to research games. The more formal consideration of games for fun through the classification of structure may well further this understanding; and experience of this process may well illuminate the relationship between these two types of game.

6.3 Game theory

One might expect to find direct parallels between game theory and gaming. It is, however, only the games played to understand, develop or use game theory that can be treated in the context of this monograph. Game theory is *not* a theory of *gaming* as discussed here. The minimax (zero-sum) game matrix and its solution provide a degenerate game, in which all initial facts, including assumptions (regarded as facts) as to how the other player will think, are open, although the actual behaviour, since it is statistical in nature, remains closed. No modifications occur, the only decision being the solution of the game which is arrived at mathematically. The game is classified

$$B (A; N; C) \cdot R (A; N; C).$$

The closure of information to the automata, imposed by the experimenter, here allows full knowledge of the value system and aims of the other player, and the C classification therefore has attributes associated with O', but without the physical states' being completely known. Game theory formalizes the notions of strategy and decision and seeks to remove the decision-process from the area of subjective judgement. In contrast, games may show what people do; they may give some idea of why; but they do not, in themselves, tell what people *should* do.

Thomas and Deemer[25] devised a submarine–air game to test the ideas of minimax strategy. The submarine and aircraft commanders separately decided on their strategies, in a very simply structured game, and, each time, one of them was judged to win in accordance with defined rules. Two players, umpired by a third person, played a sequence of 25 similar choices, with an implicit learning process. Other sequences were played with the roles changed, so that all combinations of roles were equally represented. The whole set was repeated, as required, with the same three players. These games began as

$$B (P; M; C) \cdot R (P; M; C)$$

games, with the closed nature of the game being almost total. As learning took place, the opponent's strategy became more and more apparent and the play tended towards the minimax solution predicted by game theory. In other words, as learning takes place, P approaches A, M approaches N, and the attributes normally associated with O increasingly qualify C, although none of the limits is ever reached. Results astonishingly close to the theoretical solution of the game can be achieved even by those with little knowledge of zero-sum game theory. This is known also to be true of those who, like the author, are biased against the logic of zero-sum game-theoretic representation of real-world situations. However, it seems that this game is primarily a game for fun based on a zero-sum game-theoretic concept.

Non-zero-sum game theory is more realistic because, basically, the game matrices afford no satisfactory solution to the decision-problem. The matrices, however, in many cases, model a dynamic process, and, in the real world, exploratory moves can be made. The game-theoretic approach is to seek attitudes, or behaviours, that are necessary and sufficient conditions for a mutually satisfactory compromise to be reached in the game-world. As far as theoretical study is concerned, the game is usually processed as a balance or mix between

$$B (A; N; C) \cdot R (A; N; C) \text{ and } B (A; M; O') \cdot R (A; M; O').$$

It is an abstraction of a 'game' played in real life, largely as a

$$B(P; M; O) \cdot R(P; M; O)$$

game. Such a real-world 'game' could be a peacetime political–military interaction with only intentions, prejudices, etc. hidden, like a gigantic game of Chess. The process of modification that takes place, in such a real situation, occurs as a result of reconnaissance, intelligence and communication between 'players', enabling openness of physical state to move towards openness of attitudes. It is these attitudes that the game-theoretic approach seeks to formalise.

Although the non-zero-sum and zero-sum (minimax) games are similarly classified, the aims are different. The minimax game determines, independently, the best strategies for each player, under certain assumptions. In the non-zero-sum game, the best mutual strategies may be evident, but the way of achieving such a joint strategy has to be sought.

Much has here been left unsaid. Obviously, gaming, or some equivalent experience, must lie behind the choice of data and decision-behaviours that form the matrices and rules of a game-theoretic approach. It is unimportant, if the normal scientific loop process is followed, whether theory is initially based on unstructured ideas (a flash of insight) or whether it stems from gaming experiments. The subsequent cyclic process, of theory, gaming, reconsideration of theory, and so on, is, however, very important.

It was such a scientific approach that gave the experimental gaming and game-theoretic work at the University of Pennsylvania[26] a special place in behaviour-theory research, at least in the judgement of the author. This work was the starting point for similarly directed work which began at the University of Sussex in 1973 and which is still in progress. Whereas the American studies were confined to theories developed in what Ackoff calls an 'Artificial Reality', the Sussex studies are now being based on theories culled from observation of the real world. This is not to deny the earlier logic, which implied a steady progress towards real-world theories, but to accept and by-pass the inevitable slowness of that progress. It is hoped to obtain from the Sussex work insights into behaviour which will be theoretically less certain, but valuable as a check-list or monitor for decision-makers in conflict situations[27, 28]. Although no statements will be made of what *ought* to be done in a particular situation, it is hoped to identify and list some of the feasible actions, and consequences of actions, and how these *might* be perceived by others; all of this would be offered to a decision-maker as information that he might wish to use.

If the references quoted here are read in the light of a background of earlier work, which has been summarized and referenced by Shubik[7] (and see appendix), the reader will understand the author's decision not to attempt to write a *short* coherent account of work on game theory and experimental games. That such an attempt would, at present, be confusing rather than helpful is a sufficient reason for its omission here. A further reason is that this very difficult research area is only one of a number which have theories and concepts of potential relevance to the construction and playing of games; decision theory, decision methodology, theories of communication and information, and the vast and growing literature of conflict resolution, have equal claims for consideration. The author has neither the space nor the skill to attempt to provide a total conceptual framework for future game developments. Development of theories of behaviour is difficult, and rapid progress is unlikely. Game theory will give useful support, but it is not necessarily the main, and certainly not the only, basis for what is required.

6.4 Management games

It has already been said that many intended research games of $B(P; M; C) \cdot R(P; M; C)$ type have in fact fulfilled a valuable learning function, although their explicit findings have been disappointing. Many management games are less complicated than these and, although they are still strictly learning games, it is possible to distil broad but very useful principles from them.

Kidd[29, 30] has devised an interesting $B(P; M; C) \cdot R(A; M; O)$ game, in which the 'students' start with a viable firm selling a single product and having capital available for advertising, market research, research and development, and so on. They have sources of advice which are free, but which use up valuable decision-making time. The advisers are a psychologist to advise on working styles and an OR consultant. The players work in teams and so have to make group-decisions, and they are scored at intervals according to their calculated share prices. They are aware of the game rules for assessing goodness or badness of their performance. It was apparent from playing these games that the use of advice, to help the students to model the uncertain situation with which they were faced, was a paying proposition; players were enabled to become aware that without such modelling, and some experimentation with their decision-set in order to observe the reactions of the environment, they were unlikely to choose an optimal decision-set.

In so far as these and other principles can be *taught*, this game is a teaching game and thus has some characteristics of a useful research game. It is clear that how far one can go in this direction depends on the simplicity of the particular game, on an understanding by the experimenter and the players of the relationships within the sequence of decisions made, and, of course, on the 'reality' of the game-situation for the players.

There are several games, of a similar sort, which deal with the management of a company at a senior level. Two examples are referenced: the Scottish Management Game[31], which was designed, by Mr W. C. Robertson and others, as a game for fun as well as a learning game, since it was to be played competitively by volunteer teams; and the Honeywell Management Game[32], which has been similarly played. In 1976, a 'competition' using this latter game was organised by the London and South East Operational Research Society (LASEORS), and hosted by the British American Tobacco Company at their Management Centre at Chelwood, Sussex. Some support for Kidd's findings on the value of OR advice might be claimed, since the LASEORS Committee Team won the prize, but this might equally have been the result of inherent business skill or game-playing ability.

In a private communication, Robertson has suggested that, especially after a series of games against an automaton opponent, BLUE might develop automatic approaches. In terms of the foregoing classification, he will tend towards B (A; M; O); and this tendency must generally be guarded against, whatever the purpose of the game (an exception is illustrated in comments on the Thomas–Deemer game in the preceding section). In a learning game, gamesmanship, such as deducing and taking advantage of the rules of the game (which are never other than dimly discerned in real-world situations), may not be exposed through analysis, so that in management games which individuals may play many times, special precautions may be needed.

There is little doubt of the value of management games, both to those who face the real-world situation represented in the game and to operational researchers. Eilon[33] produced, in 1963, a classification of 'business' games, based on design characteristics and purpose. This provided 30 possible categories, although some games could be placed in more than one of them. Although developed on a different basis from the classification of chapter 2, it nevertheless seems to have useful potential as a *specialized* classification. It adds to, but does not conflict with, the classifications discussed earlier. It may be noted that 'research' is quoted as one of the purposes, although no clear definition of what this implies is stated.

6.5 Further comment on the relationship between games for different purposes

Management games are learning games and may relate to research games in two ways. Firstly, they may have some teaching function; secondly, there must be a learning process in the development of research games which might need support from a learning game. A *direct* translation of learning aspects to research aspects seems unlikely. Nevertheless, attempts are to be made by the National Coal Board to develop a recently devised management game[34] into a research tool. It is of particular interest that research was the prime intention, and the learning game was consciously chosen as a first step. Experience from this game and the management support it would generate were judged to be needed before a research game (or a game which could be an exploratory tool for management planners themselves) could be developed.

The process modelled for this management game is, and has to be, detailed and realistic, both in environment and in decision-making. This will tend to operate against its becoming more than a vehicle for operational researchers, as well as managers, to learn. But judgement must be deferred, since it is possible that inherent teaching potential in parts of the game as it now exists can be developed for research purposes. It is also possible that researchers and players together may have sufficient 'feel' for the decision-sequences involved, for the game to be regarded, and controlled, as a single-decision-point game.

All learning games and research games need to have an element of fun, partly to motivate the player and partly to enable 'disaster' to be faced equably. In learning games, those who equate the game-world with the real world *too* closely could, perhaps, become too worried to learn: their mental processes could be so taken up with concern about the outcome that they would be unable to analyse, and learn from, the process that they are going through. A similar effect occurs in games for fun: the fun may disappear if real-world values are grafted onto the game (for example, concern with one's reputation as a game-player, or with loss or gain of more than a trivial amount of money). Since some serious attention to the game is necessary both for learning and for fun, there is a nice balance to be struck in both cases.

Teaching games are not supposed to be fun *per se*. They are serious business for teacher and student alike. A course of study will generally be more acceptable if it combines teaching *and* learning, in the senses defined in chapter 2. The mixture can be supplied within a single process or in separate processes of study. The learning part is a personal and chosen exploration, and it would be surprising if this were not fun for the majority. The teaching part may be as small as the directing of interest towards certain aspects of the subject under study. This is present in any management game.

There may be accidental effects of these relationships. A learning game, such as a management game, may not necessarily be a good game for its intended purpose. But it might continue to exist because players, finding it fun, expressed satisfaction. It would be useful therefore for there to be explicit teaching functions deliberately built in, since the control exercised on these would provide some check on the game's validity for its main purpose. It can certainly be argued[14] that many games, wrongly designated as research games, have had a long life simply because they were learning games which players enjoyed playing.

Finally, it is always useful, when documenting a game, to state what its purpose is and how this has affected its design. Otherwise, it may get used for some other purpose, of the same broad type, or even a different type, without appropriate modifications. It is not unkind to suggest that such misuse has often occurred. Tools which are available tend to be used, even in inappropriate ways. Operational research tools, of all kinds, are no exception.

7. Possible future developments

7.1 Some tentative conclusions

It is permissible for an author to conclude with a few unproven or not formally proven statements, and with what he sees as hopeful prospects for the future. It may even be a duty to do so. This will provide readers with some picture of biasses, preferences, and perceptions, which enables each to judge whether the arguments that have been read seem to have been unduly swayed by the author's unavoidable subjectivity, allied to his experience and his research intentions.

It is urged that, until a lot of careful research has been done, large-scale multiple-decision games should be firmly designated as learning games only. It is also seen as true that, at present, it is only through the most simple games that research in the strictest sense can be carried out. It is believed that fundamental inquiry into behavioural and informational concepts is an essential prerequisite for successful research games. Progress will inevitably be slow.

It has been seen that, provided that research concentrates on a single *decision* in a one-person game, it is possible to contemplate rich informational *environments*. Alternatively, if the environment is sufficiently simple for multiple-decision processes to be understood (see under the ARL Game in chapter 4), then these latter can be analysed. A third approach, which stems from Sharp's work[9] on the game of 'Diplomacy', referred to briefly in chapter 2, is through the possibility of feeding players 'realistically' into the same point in a pre-recorded 'game', involving a complicated prior decision-sequence which the players can accept (to an extent which can be crudely measured) as their own. If this can be extended to less formalised game structures, a move towards the development of one-person research games dealing with more than a single decision becomes possible.

Learning games for researchers is one field in which major progress might perhaps be made more quickly. It is not that such processes do not exist; but they are rarely seen clearly as games. If operational research models of some complexity, such as simulations which use probabilistic representations of decision-processes, are used in the first place as learning games, to study what the consequences of different representations might be, the research use of such models, and how their solutions can be properly used, might be better understood. This should be extended to the testing, subjectively, of whether more faithful one-to-one representation of the real world gives results which have important differences, the causes of which can be understood in the model and can be extrapolated to the real world.

It may be claimed that this is already being done. *Sensitivity testing* is the name of the game. There is a difference, however, between testing the sensitivity of a model during the 'solution' phase (that is, in the course of the advisory process), and testing it in the model development stage. It is the latter course that is proposed as a further part of the move towards a theory of choice of models. White[1], and the present author in the context of game classification[19], point to the absence of a clear basis for the choice of models. The use of games to develop understanding of the choice of models, and indeed other secondary choices, seems to be a practicable and desirable approach.

But whatever is 'right' or 'wrong', there is little doubt that gaming will continue to be enthusiastically practised, especially by operational researchers, management advisers, and teachers. This monograph has been written in the hope that it will help to enable the very considerable resources of time, money and people that are involved to be used in as profitable a way as possible. It is not implied that, at this still early stage in the development of games as research and training devices, enough is known to ensure that the best type of game is chosen for the purpose intended. Nor is it yet established that the theoretical ideas put forward on the design and control of games will be easy to put into practice. A lot will depend on the amount of research effort devoted to game development, as well as on the pragmatic and inspirational ideas which will come from game-makers working independently of any ideas put forward here. Much of what has been said may be regarded by some as common sense, and already 'known'. Even if that is so, the attempt to make it explicit and integrate it in a common framework is an essential step towards theory.

It has been very apparent to the author, seeking, over many years, for other people's ideas and experience on games, that all too little has been written up in a complete way, and that what has been written has not necessarily been very easy to understand or use, outside the context of the problem or situation for which the game was designed. A few years ago, the possibility of an OR Society Study Group on games was suggested, but it never came into being. If this monograph leads towards the setting up of such a focal point for the collection, discussion and dissemination of ideas, this alone would make its writing worth while. The International Simulation and Gaming Association (SAGA) exists for this purpose among many others, but it seems that a smaller, more closely knit group—one that would be more like an informal research team— might be more useful at this stage.

7.2 A current research programme

Certain recent developments that may lead in this direction are worth recording here. Firstly, the ideas of chapter 5 are being followed up through research at Royal Holloway College, University of London, in the Department of Mathematics (Professor M. R. C. McDowell; Research Fellow, Dr D. Cooper). The aims of this research are

(1) to determine some conflict areas which could be usefully studied and for which there is adequate access to necessary information;

(2) to define single decision-points that appear to be

H

critical in one or more of these conflict situations, and
to define the nature of these decision-points;

(3) to create, through a game process, detailed scenarios
of the chosen conflict situations as a basis for games
related to individual decisions, with information as a
controlled variable;

(4) to use these games to obtain insight into the factors that
control particular behaviours (for example, changes of
policy or aim; perception of crisis); and

(5) to investigate relevant theories of behaviour and to test
these in the game-world.

It is hoped to show that such game-playing is a practicable and relevant general method for establishing useful models of decision-
making in real-world situations. No attempt will be made to say
what decision-makers *should* do, but it is intended to establish the
attainable facilities, such as the information they can get and the
actions they can consider as options, that might make a critical
change in a decision or make decision-making 'easier'. In the development of such games, it may be possible to use the type of game
proposed by Sharp[9]. (Just before this book went to press, Cooper
reported a method which is a major advance on Sharp's. An account
will be published in the literature in due course.)

Secondly, at the University of Sussex, research is continuing
on the development of games, within a game-theoretic framework,
for the better understanding of individual behaviour in simple
situations, and for testing theories of behaviour which may be
hypothesized from real-world situations or, indeed, from environment-rich games (Professor B. P. H. R. Rivett; Research Fellow,
Dr P. G. Bennett). Earlier work by Dr M. R. Dando and students
under his direction (which led to the acceptance of this work as
'operational research' and to its support by the Science Research
Council) has already been mentioned[27, 28]. The research at Sussex
University and that at Royal Holloway College will be co-ordinated
by informal exchanges and by their links with a third research study
on organizational structure (which will also eventually need gaming
of some sort). This last study will be carried out by Dr Dando

and the author's research group at the Defence Operational Analysis Establishment, and may well develop some of the ideas of section 4.4.6 to shed light on how to analyse the conflicts that may occur between parts of a real organization. A more complete statement of their total research programme has been given elsewhere[35].

A third area of game development centres on the Home Office which has been developing and using games in the context of forward planning for handling large-scale civil disasters, whether of natural or man-made origin. So far, some simple but most effective learning games have been produced through work at the Royal Military College of Science (Professor R. W. Shephard; Research Fellow, Dr P. V. Johnson). The development of research games for the same or analogous types of situation has recently been under discussion. This is, at present, quite independent of the programme described above, but there is a strong mutual interest in collaboration to whatever extent proves possible.

7.3 Public participation in social planning

Other work known to be in progress is the development of a Strategic Choice Game (Joyce and Sinclair[36, 37]). This is being carried out at the University of Aston in the context of environmental planning, and seems to be following a line of inquiry which is similar in some respects to that described in section 7.2. The game will be used to present members of the public with various representations of the broad issues facing planners and to seek responses, especially preferences between actions and deployment of resources, to meet the social needs of the population of an area. The most important purpose of the research is

'to test hypotheses regarding the presence, and structure, of internal representation of strategic environments/ environmental processes in respondents, and subsequent to administering (the game) to test hypotheses regarding the effect of (the game), i.e. its form and information content, on those internal representations'.[36]

H 2

It is observed that the interaction between a subject's internal cognitive processes and the survey techniques is of great importance in research into the use of social survey techniques in eliciting response to strategic environmental issues: how does 'information' and the way in which it is presented, together with the personal framework of understanding and the motivation of the individual, affect the choice made? An important question is being asked, namely what is the information content, for a particular individual in a particular choice situation as perceived by him, of a known set of data? There are difficulties in measuring information in these terms, and the limitations imposed on the understanding of decision-processes are themselves not yet well understood[10, 38].

Whether or not the research intentions of this study succeed, the game is certain to provide a valuable learning activity for the planner in interaction with the people whom, ultimately, he is serving. A similar learning process applies for those members of the public who participate. Through this mutual learning process much confusion and conflict may be avoided.

This attitude is part of the argument for games put by Mackie[39] to a conference on architectural psychology. He gives references to several uses by 'human scientists' of gaming, or the concept of a game, as an analogue of human activity in social situations. However, he indicates, quoting Raser[40], that, in the social sciences, there has not been much use of research games. The games played are, generally, 'free' games (all modifications allowed). Of his own work in urban design, he describes the Aberdeen Environmental Game which is an Instructional Simulation (AEGIS). At the time of the conference, 1973, he reported proposals to develop the game 'to involve local planners and public groups in a negotiative dialogue'.

AEGIS provides a physical three-dimensional model of a town, and, in any game, all the problems of extracting decision-processes from a rich environment, and understanding them, will apply. A preliminary experiment, however, has generated design information from a game involving smaller-scale housing layouts; this early game was chosen as an alternative to a questionnaire, because the latter approach was believed to introduce biases and to provide inadequate background information. Although it is not implied that research of the type proposed by Joyce and Sinclair is intended at Aberdeen, it is encouraging to note that there was success both in creating an atmosphere of trust and in encouraging two-way communication.

The present author has not yet had the opportunity to follow up the uses of gaming for such public participation, and the Aberdeen work (at the Scott Sutherland School of Architecture) may have advanced into further interesting game applications. It is reported here to emphasize that learning games played by researchers (or planners) are beginning to assume a potential role of some social importance.

7.4 A science based on games?

It may well be that, in many other research groups and institutions, including those for which games have already proved useful in the past, basic research is being proposed or new games, for research purposes, are being developed. If the past is any guide, only a small part of the work done will be published, or become known informally in any detail to other workers in the field. The same concern has been voiced by Shubik[4] (see appendix 2). Perhaps, despite the private enthusiasm of all who play games, the reasons for detailed communication are not yet seen as compelling.

If, however, readers are prepared to accept views recently put forward by Dando, Defrenne and Sharp[41], a more urgent case is made. Dando and his colleagues question the whole future of operational research, which they refer to as a technology which will remain a hit-and-miss affair, unless an underlying science can be developed. Such a science would have, as the phenomena of concern, the decision-making processes in organizations. The language of the science would be drawn from systems theories (for example, Ackoff and Emery[10]), and theory-testing would be associated with developments of decision-methodology[1] and with controlled forms of gaming.

This choice of games, as a fundamental tool for experimental work, stems from the essential behavioural content of any complete study of large-scale problems[35], and the consequent need to model people and their decision-behaviour. Shubik[7] comments on the future of gaming in ways which are not inconsistent with the ideas expressed by Dando and his colleagues. Perhaps, therefore, the way ahead may soon be able to be seen more clearly than an examination of the present overall conduct of gaming might suggest. If such a direction can be agreed, and if moves in that direction take place, the games that children play may pay dividends when, as adults, they join the battle to study and control the world in which we live.

Appendix. American literature on games

A.1 Introduction

As stated in section 1.5, this monograph has concentrated on attitudes towards games, and on the games played, in the United Kingdom. In particular, it records work done by the author and his colleagues on the classification of games as an aid to choosing the type of game to be played, and on the establishing of principles for the design and control of games. This, however, would be less than adequate without pointing to similar work in the United States. The use of games in the United States over the years has been far more extensive than elsewhere, and it would be wasteful to ignore either the positive or negative lessons that can be drawn from this experience.

In recent years, most valuable summaries of United States gaming have appeared, due mainly to the efforts of Professor M. Shubik of Yale University. In 1970–71, working as a consultant to the RAND Corporation, he took the leading role in the production of three reports which surveyed the usefulness, the scientific nature, and the literature of gaming[4–6]. There followed, in 1975, two books[7, 8] which cover, with very full references, both theoretical and practical aspects of the subject.

It will be evident to those who read these publications that some of the views expressed are similar to, or at least not in conflict with, those already expressed here. But there are dissimilarities and differences in approach, such as those briefly discussed in chapter 2, and further points will be made in the summaries and discussions that follow. Whether these dissimilarities are the sort of disparities that must occur when different cross-sections are taken of a vast multi-dimensional, and still ill-understood, subject, or whether they represent substantial issues, is not a question that can be usefully addressed here. The best advice to readers is that they should take what they perceive to be of most value from all they read and continue to merge ideas into a new and improved framework. In this way, the phrases used in the introductory chapter—'an approach to a theory of games'—and in the subtitle of one of Shubik's books—*Towards a Theory of Gaming*—can begin to take on an operational meaning.

The five sections that follow are headed with the titles of the Shubik references and comprise a summary of and a commentary on them.

A.2 Models, simulations and games: a survey

This report[4] gives the results of a survey by questionnaire of a sample of the models, simulations and games (MSG) used by the US Department of Defense and its agencies. The sample size was 132. The aim of the survey was to get an overall picture of the purposes, use, benefits and costs of such analysis procedures, and to provide standard descriptions and classifications to assist in the interchange of information on the characteristics of existing MSG; to provide an aid to the construction of, and to the estimation of the characteristics of, new MSG; and to enable evaluation of past and current activities to take place.

The conclusions and recommendations cannot easily be summarised, since there are important qualifications, and many factors of contextual relevance to the understanding of such conclusions. But, briefly, concern was expressed on five main points.

(a) The quality and the scientific rigour of the production of MSG were inadequate.

(b) Large-scale, finely detailed MSG cannot, in general, be seen as reliable, valid or successful.

(c) Too many MSG are *not* subjected to sensitivity tests, nor are their input data and assumptions adequately defined, documented and tested.

(d) Professional communication of what is done, why, and with what success, is poor.

(e) Studies of the costs, in money and manpower, of providing MSG, in relation to their estimated usefulness, are few in number.

Not all of these findings related specifically to non-degenerate games. Of the findings on games with human players, it was recommended that more attention be given to the development of games (of a large-scale nature) for teaching and training. The comment at (b) above implies that they were not generally suited for defence operational research. Following a brief examination of gaming in the civilian sector, fears were expressed that many of the mistakes committed in applying games and simulation to defence problems were about to be repeated in civil-sector applications, which were seen to be growing at an appreciable rate.

A.3 The literature of gaming, simulation and model-building: index and critical abstracts

This report is no ordinary bibliography. It indexes each paper or book under thirteen separate headings. The index uses multiple categories where such use is relevant and aids description. The headings are as follows.

(1) Whether abstracted by the author, not abstracted, abstracted by the bibliographers or specially reviewed by them.

(2) Nature of content—whether it is only broadly related to games, is a generalized or abstract discussion of games, or is a paper on specific game description, documentation or results.

(3) Security classification.

(4) Source of funding.

(5) Name of gaming organization (if applicable).

(6) Name of game (if applicable).

(7) Mathematical sophistication (five levels, 'none' to 'high').

(8) Purpose (entertainment; experimental; operational; popularization, advocacy; research/theory development; teaching; training).

(9) Qualitative assessment ('not evaluated', or one of five levels, 'excellent' to 'bad').

(10) RAND publication or otherwise (note that most of the literature comes from RAND).

(11) Subject (for example, Artificial Intelligence, Business, Game Theory, Gaming Theory/Methodology, Political Science, Urban Planning, War Gaming).

(12) Type of publication.

(13) Year of publication.

In a sense, the most interesting part of the report is the judgement of the bibliographers on 'limited use' or 'bad' literature and on what they have chosen as 'excellent'. The original account of the classification discussed in chapter 4 was classified as 'modal' and, at the time, the present author would have (reluctantly!) seen this as a fair comment. However, since then, the use made of this classification would lead him to raise its category by one degree. The classification has in fact been instrumental in structuring inquiries into what sort of game should be played for a particular research purpose; in bringing together the ideas for games of equivalent or near equivalent types; and, in particular, in making explicit the importance of what are still seen as some of the key variables in a game (additional important variables are those discussed in chapter 5). This is mentioned to illustrate that a critical bibliography, such as this, is bound to need updating, since qualitative assessments of value are bound to change as the subject develops. This does not mean that in this case either the present author or Professor Shubik is correct. The important issue is that the value of ideas is not absolute over time.

As a further illustration of how the indexing is used, other categorizations of the chapter 4 material on the classification of games are

Mathematical sophistication	— 'Slight'
Purpose	— 'Operational'
Type	— 'General/abstract discussion'
Subject	— 'Gaming theory/methodology'

With none of this could there be any disagreement for the purposes of Shubik's bibliography. It may, however, be worth noting, for those who may wish to extend or use the ideas in his report, that ideas of mathematical sophistication depend on the definition of mathematics. The classification and set-theoretic approaches to description which have been used in this monograph are themselves mathematical in principle, and are very much more 'sophisticated' than would appear to the conventional mathematical eye. In seeking understanding of gaming processes, it may well be that a realisation of underlying structures will help as much as elaborate mathematical theory. It could therefore be useful to subdivide both the 'none' and 'slight' mathematical sophistication categories into the use or non-use of structural/logical processes of a formal nature.

None of this is intended as special pleading. It is instructive to an author to consider the classification and rating of his own work in relation to other work in the same field. More importantly, an author can then consider what would need to be added to improve the value of his work as seen by others. These others do not have the sort of information that an author has (but which he may not yet be able, or may not wish, to make explicit) about how he has used his own work in communicating with his colleagues. If such a reviewing classification were a common practice, authors might become more explicit in relation to some of the headings and categories used in it, and they would also have reason to help to extend the classification and make it more useful, at least as a *comparative* description of the books and papers reviewed.

A.4 Review of selected books and articles on gaming and simulation

These[6] are the 'special reviews' indexed under the first heading of the foregoing literature survey. They are forthright and, in the words of the reviewers, 'contain value judgements, whose merits will ultimately rest on our professional competence'. Shubik and his colleagues recommend a Delphi-type process for reviewing, to redress what they regard as built-in constraints on reviewers, who are not encouraged by the present procedures 'to say that a book is bad or to identify as mediocre the results of a sincere but half-baked idea'.

The reviews cover the range 'bad' to 'excellent'. From his knowledge of some of the literature described the present author concludes that the reviewers have given a valuable service. It may be added that British literature reviewers do not seem to be inhibited in the way that, it is implied, is typical in the United States.

A.5 Games for society, business and war: towards a theory of gaming

Shubik describes this book[7] as an overall survey of gaming. It is a survey of a very special type, since half of the book is devoted to providing a background to the theory of games. It is accepted that the latter is a completely different topic, but that, nevertheless, the concepts of game theory are of value to any type of game. The reasons for this statement are many and they appear explicitly and implicitly throughout the book.

There is, first, the fact that game-theoretic formulations are 'environment poor', so that the concepts and principles of a two-person interaction can more easily be discerned; the formal structure itself provides a clarity which might be submerged in the richness of the more general game scenario. Thus, attention is drawn to such features as the information conditions, the briefing of the players, the nature of the rules, the possible strategies, the presentation and aggregations of the game, and the role of chance. From time to time, there seems to be some uncertainty as to whether it is a game-theoretic formulation that is under consideration, or a simple experimental game (to study behaviour) played using a game-theoretic format. However, to some extent, these can be alternative ways of getting the same kind of insight. Further, it is stressed that concepts such as pay-offs and preferences, solution of the game, and equilibria have importance in all gaming situations, as do the types of game-theoretic situations which are conceptually faced in more realistic 'environment-rich' situations. Zero-sum game theory is only briefly mentioned, since there is no easy parallel to this in the social, political and economic environments which games are, in general, used to study.

The possible interplay between games and game theory (with the latter used in experimental games to test broad hypotheses about behaviour culled from the richer environments of the former) is not explicitly treated. However, there does not seem to be any inconsistency between the research proposals summarized in chapter 7 of this monograph, and the inferences that can be drawn by linking Shubik's summary of game theory with his separate discussions of behavioural models and of the specific uses of games in experimental social psychology.

This first half of the book might indeed be looked at as a learning game. Shubik, whether by intention or otherwise, has not offered a prescriptive treatment of the game-theory and gaming link, but has provided a most thoughtful framework within which game-makers may question their judgements, asking themselves how far they are on the road to theory or how much of their efforts is unstructured fun. Exercises, which are provided at the end of most of the early chapters, are mainly open-ended questions asking for discussion, often in a broader framework, of points arising from game-theoretic treatments. They are reminiscent of the far-reaching exercises that White[1] provides for decision-methodology studies. They suggest that this book would be a useful basis for teaching (perhaps 'learning under guidance' would be a more appropriate expression).

The second half of the book provides statistics on, and information about, games and game playing. The classification under which games are discussed here seems to be somewhat erratic and has some of the disadvantages which have been discussed in chapter 2 of this monograph; this applies also to the book discussed in section A.6. There is information on sports, which seems somewhat out of place, although it is interesting to see where the money goes. In case anyone should think that the cost of operational games (mainly large military and political games) has been excessive (ignoring any questions of the relevance of these games) it is noted that in 1971, in the United States, the money spent was about equal to the gross sales of the well-known board game, Monopoly®.

Some of the stringent comments on large-scale games are worth quoting. TEMPER[42] is described as a game which 'modestly offered a simulation of over 110 nations together with literally thousands of unverified parameters and no sensitivity analysis'. It is noted that this 'was probably not important because the model contained logical inconsistencies'. This game was studied by the present author in 1968 and was regarded as having no possible value, even as a learning game. The Internation Simulation[43] (which the present author studied in 1968 with a sort of fascinated horror) is referred to as a model which 'attempts to provide a sufficiently well-defined structure that, if one is careful, at least it is possible to consider it as a device with which some questions concerning theory building and testing can be raised'. In practice, as is made clear, the care was not taken and false analogies were used in the interpretation of results. Part of this falsity stemmed from the mismatch between players' real-world and game roles. As is remarked in another context, 'when high school students play at being the Chinese foreign minister in a highly aggregated game, they may end up with an utterly false impression of the problems of implementation of policy'.

Shubik gives a useful warning about the dangers of designing a game for one purpose and using it for another. This leads him to a final discussion on what game-makers should be designing for—what the future of gaming is. He places emphasis on correcting two perceived shortcomings in present practice—namely the lack of experimental or theoretical development by organizations where games are used for operational purposes, and the inadequate communication between individuals variously concerned with theory, experiment and operational use. It is indeed strange that scientists, who are the main developers of games, can be so blind to the absence of the basic scientific approach, namely the testing of hypotheses through experiment, the reformulation of these hypotheses, the collection of new data, retesting and so on. Shubik comments on the future place of gaming within systems science (or operational research), and he ends with an optimistic view of 'the development of a theory of gaming as a multidisciplinary approach, which provides a theoretical basis for fruitful applications of gaming to operations, teaching and experimentation, a development which provides guidance for the delicate tasks involved in the study of, prediction of, and introspection about human behaviour'.

His book will undoubtedly provide some impetus away from the unsatisfactory past, and it does indeed deserve its subtitle *Towards A Theory of Gaming*.

A.6 The uses and methods of gaming

This is a handbook[8] on how to set up, cost, and run games, and on where to find the basic literature. It repeats some of the material in the other documents summarised above but with a different emphasis. It may be regarded as a companion volume to *Games for Society, Business and War*.

The classification of games is based on their use and follows the lines of an earlier paper[11], which was discussed briefly in chapter 2 of this monograph. Shubik mentions the different approach of the present author but his reference to an earlier informal document is incorrect. It should have been Working Paper CC5 *not* Memorandum 7117 (see the Foreword to this monograph); the Defence Operational Analysis Establishment is correctly given as the source, but has been wrongly situated in Washington, DC.

Shubik's main purposes for his classification are to stress the importances of purpose and of the devising of criteria to judge what is attained; to draw attention to the common sources of knowledge and skills relevant to all gaming activity; and to suggest that the common features of the different types of game imply a need for communication between those who play games, irrespective of whether their purpose is the same or not. Some of the issues discussed under the headings *Techniques*, *Modelling and Languages*, *Costs and Procedures*, and *Facilities* could, of course, be extended both by relating them to the basic purposes of gaming and also by relating them to the more detailed purposes that lead to the choice of a particular structure for the game. Although the text does indicate that there is a wide range of games that might be played it deals mainly with the more complex end of this spectrum. This could both encourage those who need learning games rich in environmental detail, and discourage those who require control over a research game and its analysis. The present scarcity of games, particularly operational research games, which have been planned economically (for limited objectives), seems to be the reason for any apparent imbalance in the coverage that Shubik provides.

The chapter on *Intention, Specification, Control and Validation* is a most valuable discussion, not least in its concern with the relationship between the experimenter and the players. The provision of an adequate game-environment for players, and attention to sociological and social–psychological aspects, are issues all too often overlooked in games for operational purposes. Many of the factors discussed in chapter 5 of this monograph, in relation to a research game, are touched upon in this chapter. It would be most valuable, at a later date, to take games of different complexities and purposes (preferably ones which have been moderately successful), and use Shubik's arguments to reach judgements both on the final choice of game and on the way (if documented) by which that choice was arrived at. It may also be possible to take some of the points which he makes on some of the important choices about different facets of the game, as indicating potential variables for the enlargement of the classification of chapter 4 of this monograph. (This would be additional to the extensions already suggested in that chapter.) It would be a major, albeit a difficult, step forward in decision methodology and another move towards a theory of choice of models.

Shubik's final five chapters return to earlier ideas which he and his colleagues at RAND have expressed[5, 6]. The total survey of the gaming literature which is provided cannot but be valuable to anyone coming new to the field, and will perhaps be no less valuable to 'experts'. The comments are sometimes congratulatory and sometimes scathing: it is worth noting that through his many writings, Shubik has so exposed his own attitudes to gaming that his 'subjective' judgements of others can be reasonably assessed within one's own value system.

In this and in Shubik's other work, gaming is discussed as a particular variant of other types of modelling, in the same way that chapter 4 of this monograph regards computer simulations and mathematical models as having, in many cases, a close kinship with games involving human players. It is not therefore surprising that what is offered is not solely an account of games, their uses and their methods. Indeed, there is more than a hint that the reasons for playing games may be much more fundamental than is often realised. The closing paragraphs of the final chapter of this monograph offer a suggestion as to what these reasons might be.

References

1. D. J. White (1975). *Decision Methodology; a Formulation of the OR Process.* Wiley, London.
2. H. G. Wells (1970). *Little Wars* (Facsimile Reproduction). Arms and Armour Press, London.
3. C. Farman (1970). The War Game—then and now, *Illustrated London News*, 29 August, 1970.
4. M. Shubik and G. D. Brewer (1972). *Models, Simulations and Games —A Survey*, R-1060-ARPA/RC, RAND Corporation, Santa Monica, California.
5. M. Shubik, G. Brewer and E. Savage (1972). The Literature of Gaming, Simulation and Model-Building: Index and Critical Abstracts, R-620-ARPA, RAND Corporation, Santa Monica, California.
6. M. Shubik and G. D. Brewer (1972). *Reviews of Selected Books of Gaming and Simulation*, R-732-ARPA, RAND Corporation, Santa Monica, California.
7. M. Shubik (1975). *Games for Society, Business and War; Towards a Theory of Gaming.* Elsevier, New York.
8. M. Shubik (1975). *The Uses and Methods of Gaming.* Elsevier, New York.
9. R. G. Sharp and M. R. Dando (1977). The Intelligence Man System: an Approach to assisting Managers in Complex Conflicts, *Eur. J. OR*, **1.**
10. R. L. Ackoff and F. E. Emery (1972). *On Purposeful Systems; an Interdisciplinary Analysis of Individual and Social Behaviour as a System of Purposeful Events.* Tavistock, London.
11. M. Shubik (1972). On the Scope of Gaming, *Mgmt Sci.*, **18,** 5, part 2.
12. K. C. Bowen and D. G. Smith (1976). Development of models for application to conflict problems. In *The Use of Models in the Social Sciences* (ed. L. Collins). Tavistock, London.
13. E. M. L. Beale (1961). *The Role of Gaming in Military Operational Research*, DOR Admiralty, Memorandum No. 190.

14. J. Clayton Thomas and G. McNicholls (1969). *Why People Play Games; Report of a Survey*, Joint National Meeting of the American Aeronautical and Operational Research Societies, Denver, Colorado.
15. R. W. Shephard (1963). War Gaming as a Technique in the Study of Operational Research Problems. *Opl Res. Q.*, **14**, 2.
16. M. G. Weiner (1959). *War Gaming Methodology*, RM-2413, RAND Corporation, Santa Monica, California.
17. W. L. Archer and L. J. Byrne (1964). Operational Gaming and the Land Battle, *Can. OR Soc. J.*, **12**, 1.
18. R. P. Rose and P. M. Sutcliffe (1971). *Submarine Approach; A Game Technique for Target Recognition Devices*, Defence Operational Analysis Establishment (Information can be obtained from the authors; although no written papers are available, some aspects are considered in reference 19).
19. K. C. Bowen (1973). Models and decision processes. In *The Role and Effectiveness of Theories of Decision in Practice* (ed. D. J. White and K. C. Bowen (1976)), Proceedings of a Conference held in Luxembourg in August, 1973, under the aegis of the NATO Science Committee, Hodder and Stoughton, London.
20. D. J. White (1971). *The Use of Operational Gaming in Planning the Working of a Coal Mine*, a paper presented to a colloquium on Statistical Model Building, Production and Control, organized jointly by the Operational Research Society and the Institution of Electrical Engineers.
21. G. Mallen (1969). SIMPOL: The Development of Simulation Models of a Police (CID) Team, *Police Research Bulletin No. 11* (also reported at a Symposium on Instructional Simulation Systems in Higher Education, held at Birmingham University and in the *New Scientist*, 16 January, 1969).
22. D. Hicks (1976). The Management of the 120-Bed Clinical Nursing Units: an account of Research Carried Out in the Five Years 1970–1974 (Part 2, Chapter 11), Wessex Regional Health Authority, Winchester (see also *Nursing Mirror*, 3 October, 1974, pp. 71–73).
23. J. I. Harris (1974). *Some Concepts of a Conflict Game*, DOAE Memorandum M7420, Defence Operational Analysis Establishment, West Byfleet.
24. J. H. Conway (1976). *On Numbers and Games*. London Mathematical Monographs No. 6, Academic Press, New York.
25. J. Clayton Thomas and W. L. Deemer (1957). The Role of Operational Gaming in Operational Research. *J. Ops Res. Soc. Am.*, **5**, 1.

26. J. R. Emshoff and R. L. Ackoff (1970). Explanatory Models of Interactive Choice Behaviour, *Conflict Resolution*, **14**, 1.

27. M. R. Dando and A. J. Bee (1977). *Operational Research for Complex Conflicts; A Gaming Methodology for the Development of a Decision-Making Monitor, Opl Res. Q.*, **28**, 4, i.

28. C. S. Huxman, M. V. Lozowski and M. R. Dando (1977). *The Golden Age of Mixed-Motive Gaming? An Enquiry into a New Gaming Paradigm* (to be published). An earlier paper is an MSc Dissertation by the first two authors (OR Department, University of Sussex).

29. J. B. Kidd (1973). Task complexity and the performance of decision makers. In *The Role and Effectiveness of Theories of Decision in Practice* (ed. D. J. White and K. C. Bowen (1976)), Proceedings of a Conference held in Luxembourg in August 1973, under the aegis of the NATO Science Committee, Hodder and Stoughton, London.

30. J. B. Kidd (1974). *Management Games can show that OR helps Aspiring Managers*, Working Paper Series, No. 28, The University of Aston Management Centre, Birmingham.

31. EDIT.515 (1976). The Scottish Management Game, sponsored by *The Scotsman* et al., The Scotsman Publications Limited, Edinburgh.

32. HIS (1972). A Management Experience: Case Study, Management Education Services, Honeywell Information Systems Ltd.

33. S. Eilon (1963). Management Games, *Opl Res. Q.*, **14**, 2.

34. R. Bodle (1976). *The Development of the Colliery Game*, OR710/16/6, and *The Development of the Colliery Model*, OR710/36/1, OR710/37/1, informal papers, Operational Research Executive, National Coal Board, Harrow, Middlesex.

35. K. C. Bowen and J. I. Harris (1976). Problems with People: Conflict, Decision, Language and Measurement. In *Environmental Assessment of Socio-Economic Systems* (ed. D. F. Burkhardt and W. H. Ittelson (1978)), NATO Conference Series, Series II. *Systems Science*, Volume 3, Proceedings of a Conference held in Istanbul, Turkey, in October 1976, under the aegis of the NATO Science Committee. Plenum, New York.

36. F. E. Joyce and C. W. Sinclair (1976). Environmental Planning and Social Response at the Strategy Level. In *Environmental Assessment of Socio-Economic Systems* (see reference 35).

37. F. E. Joyce and C. W. Sinclair (1976). *Comments on the Form and Content of the Strategy Choice Game (SCG)*. An appendix to reference 36 (not being published), Joint Unit for Research on the Urban Environment, University of Aston, Birmingham.

38. A. Stratton and K. C. Bowen (1977). *The Information Content of Data.* Defence Operational Analysis Establishment, West Byfleet (to be published).
39. D. Mackie (1973). Gaming as a research tool in architectural psychology. In *Architectural Psychology; Proceedings of the Lund Conference* (ed. R. Küller), Dowden, Hutchinson and Ross, Inc., Stroudsburg, Pennsylvania.
40. J. R. Raser (1969). *Simulation and Society; an Exploration of Scientific Gaming.* Allyn and Bacon, Boston.
41. M. R. Dando, A. Defrenne and R. G. Sharp (1977). Could OR be a science? *OMEGA*, **5**, 1.
42. Raytheon Company (1965). *TEMPER*, Vols. I–VII, Raytheon Co., Bedford, Massachusetts.
43. H. Guetzkow (1963). *Simulation in International Relations.* Prentice-Hall, Englewood Cliffs, New Jersey.

Index